Art Activities for the
English Language Classroom

Art Activities for the English Language Classroom

Theresa Catalano

CAMBRIA
PRESS

Youngstown, New York

Copyright 2006   Theresa Catalano
All rights reserved
Printed in the United States of America
No part of this publication may be reproduced, stored in or introduced into
a retrieval system, or transmitted, in any form, or by any means (electronic,
mechanical, photocopying, recording, or otherwise), without the prior
permission of the publisher. Requests for permission should be directed to
permissions@cambriapress.com, or mailed to Permissions, Cambria Press,
PO Box 350, Youngstown, New York 14174-0350.
This book has been registered with the Library of Congress.
Catalano, Theresa
        Art Activities for the English Language Classroom / Theresa Catalano
        p. cm.

        Includes bibliographical references
        ISBN10: 1-934043-05-2
        ISBN13: 978-1-934043-05-9

To my sister Rosetta for her incredible talent and endless support.
To my children Isabella, Lorenzo, and Valentina for inspiring me.
To my parents, for their help and advice.
And to my wonderful husband, Luigi.
Ti amo!

Contents

Introduction xv
    Introduction to the Creation of Art Language Learning Technique xv
    How Does it Work? xv
    Helpful Conversation Tips for Classroom Art Activities xvii
    Helpful Art Tips for Classroom Art Activities xix
    How to Use This Book xix

Chapter One: Vocabulary Activities 1
    1.1   Colors/Animals/Classroom Objects 2
    1.2   Time 3
    1.3   Family 4
    1.4   Days of the week 6
    1.5   Feelings 7
    1.6   Describing People 8
    1.7   Occupations 9
    1.8   Food 11
    1.9   Body parts 12
    1.10   Sports 14
    1.11   Weather/Months 15
    1.12   Clothing 16
    1.13   City locations 17
    1.14   Dance Line 19
    1.15   Transportation 20
    1.16   Human Art Bingo 21
    1.17   Relay 22
    1.18   Swat the Flies 23

Chapter Two: Reading Activities 27
    2.1   One Minute Story 27
    2.2   Re-Tell the Story 28
    2.3   Main Idea 29
    2.4   Main Characters 30
    2.5   Art Jigsaw 32
    2.6   Half and Half 33
    2.7   Scrambled Reading 34

Chapter Three: Writing Activities 37
    3.1   Half and Half writing 37
    3.2   General Story Writing 39
    3.3   Art Missing Words Dictacomp 40
    3.4   Student Art Dictacomp 41
    3.5   What's Different? 42
    3.6   Wanted Criminals 43
    3.7   Abstractions 44
    3.8   Three Part Story 46

Chapter Four: Grammar 49
    4.1   Simple Present 49
    4.2   Be/Have 51
    4.3   Present Progressive—Picture Descriptions 52
    4.4   Present Progressive—Imagine 53
    4.5   Simple Past 54
    4.6   Simple Past—An Embarrassing Thing That Happened 55
    4.7   Past Progressive 56
    4.8   Verb Tense Review—Remember the Song 58
    4.9   Present Perfect 59
    4.10   Future—Future Progressive 60
    4.11   Future—What Happens Next? 61
    4.12   Review of Tenses 63
    4.13   Questions 64
    4.14   Questions—Commercials 65
    4.15   Count/Non-count 67
    4.16   Prepositions 68
    4.17   Error Analysis 70
    4.18   Adjectives 71
    4.19   Modals 73
    4.20   Passive 74
    4.21   Comparatives/Superlatives 75
    4.22   Comparatives/Works of Art 77
    4.23   Comparatives/Superlatives "The Bachelor/The Bachelorette" 78
    4.24   Simple Past Review 79
    4.25   Making Suggestions/Giving Compliments 81
    4.26   Conditionals—Untrue (Contrary to Fact) in the Present/Future ... 82

Chapter Five: Speaking 85
5.1 Speaking Chain 85
5.2 Conversation Line With a Picture 87
5.3 Beginning, Middle, and End 88
5.4 What Happened in the Picture? 89
5.5 Categories 90
5.6 What am I? 91
5.7 Self-Portraits 92
5.8 Art Show 93
5.9 Puppet Show 95
5.10 T.V. Talk 96
5.11 Let's Talk Politics 97
5.12 International Inventor 99

Chapter Six: Listening 103
6.1 Re-Create the Picture 103
6.2 Math problems 105
6.3 Re-Tell the story 107
6.4 Draw What I Say 108
6.5 Art Installation 109

References 111

About the Author 113

Credits 115

Activities According to Level

Beginning
1.3 Family 4
1.4 Days of the Week 6
1.13 City Locations 17
4.1 Simple Present 49
4.3 Present Progressive—Picture Descriptions 52
4.4 Present Progressive—Imagine 53

Beginning-Intermediate

1.1	Colors/Animals/Classroom Objects	2
1.2	Time	3
1.7	Occupations	9
1.8	Food	11
1.9	Body Parts	12
1.10	Sports	14
1.11	Weather/Months	15
1.15	Transportation	20
3.5	What's Different?	42
3.6	Wanted Criminals	43
3.7	Abstractions	44
4.2	Be/Have	49
4.15	Count/Non-Count	67
4.16	Prepositions	68
4.21	Comparatives/Superlatives	75
5.7	Self-Portraits	92
6.1	Re-Create the Picture	103

Beginning-Intermediate-Advanced

1.5	Feelings	7
1.6	Describing People	8
1.16	Human Art Bingo	21
1.17	Relay	22
1.18	Swat the Flies	23
2.4	Main Characters	30
2.7	Scrambled Reading	34
3.3	Art Missing Words Dictacomp	40
3.4	Student Art Dictacomp	41
4.13	Questions	64
4.18	Adjectives	71
5.6	What Am I?	91
5.8	Art Show	93
5.9	Puppet Show	95
6.4	Draw What I Say	108
6.5	Art Installation	109

Intermediate

4.5	Simple Past	54
4.10	Future—Future Progressive	60
4.11	Future—What Happens Next?	61
4.17	Error Analysis	70
4.19	Modals	73

Intermediate-Advanced

1.7	Clothing	9
2.3	Main Idea	29
2.5	Art Jigsaw	32
2.6	Half and Half	33
3.1	Half and Half Writing	37
3.2	General Story Writing	39
3.5	Three Part Story	42
4.6	Simple Past—An Embarrassing Thing That Happened	55
4.7	Past Progressive	56
4.8	Verb Tense Review—Remember the Song	58
4.9	Present Perfect	59
4.14	Questions—Commercials	65
4.22	Comparatives/Works of Art	77
4.23	Comparatives/Superlatives "The Bachelor/The Bachelorette"	78
4.24	Simple Past Review	79
4.25	Making Suggestions/Giving Compliments	81
4.26	Conditionals/Untrue (Contrary to Fact) in the Present/Future	82
5.1	Speaking Chain	85
5.2	Conversation Line With a Picture	87
5.3	Beginning, Middle, and End	88
5.4	What Happened in the Picture?	89
5.5	Categories	90
5.10	T.V. Talk	96
5.12	International Inventor	99

Advanced

2.2	Re-Tell the Story	28
4.12	Review of Tenses	63
4.20	Passive	74
5.11	Let's Talk Politics	97

Foreword

Teachers in the classroom today are aware of the different ways students learn, but they often find it difficult to incorporate multiple learning styles or "intelligences" into their lessons. This book addresses that need for language teachers with clever, simple-to-do, activities at a variety of student levels. Through art making activities Ms. Catalano gets students actively involved in their language learning, using visual, auditory and kinesthetic senses in all the lessons. Instructions are clear and there are many easy lessons dealing with vocabulary, reading, grammar, writing, speaking and listening. Many of these lessons can be added to the existing curriculum with very little effort on the teacher's part. A teacher can incorporate several of these lessons as desired and introduce students to the practice gradually or can transform the entire course with these activities.

Those of us who have traveled in a country in which another language is spoken know that to really learn a language you must live it. To be immersed in a language you see it, hear it and begin to think in it. These activities help students begin to experience this in the typical American classroom. Students draw and act as they speak the target language; they play games, create projects and interact with one another through the target language. The constant interaction between the visual, the verbal, and the kinesthetic makes this possible.

As an art educator, I have been helping teachers for many years to incorporate art making and art history into other areas of study. Art can often be a motivator for students and help them to become more engaged in their learning. It provides another avenue for students to excel and thus succeed in their education. In the activities provided in this book, art provides a way for students to use their visual memory to aid in their language acquisition and for students to physically create images while they verbally practice language skills.

The activities provided here vary in their complexity from having students make quick sketches to aid in vocabulary acquisition to working as a group to create an installation that will immerse others in the target language. High school teachers might extend this final lesson by collaborating with their art specialists to have students study installations made by professional artists and thus learn more about art as they work with language learning. Ms. Catalano has created numerous activities that will inspire teachers to make their classrooms active, creative and fun and will inspire students to learn.

Dr. Joanne Sowell
Associate Professor of Art History
University of Nebraska at Omaha

Acknowledgements

Many thanks to my family and friends for all their encouragement and support. Special thanks to my friends and colleagues at the University of Nebraska, Creighton Preparatory School, and Metro Community College for their excellent advice, input, and enthusiasm. Special thanks also to my excellent professors from the University of Arizona who taught me so much about how to teach better and prepare less. Thanks also to Juliette Henning for bringing art back into my life.

Introduction

Why Use the **Creation of Art** Language Learning Technique?

Language learners are all different and learn in different ways. **The **Auditory** learners prefer oral directions over written and acquire knowledge by reading aloud. They remember by verbalizing lessons to themselves. **Visual** learners like to see what they are learning. They benefit from illustrations and presentations that use color and are attracted to written or spoken language rich in imagery. **Kinesthetic** learners rely on what they can directly experience or perform. They need to be active, and remember what was done, but have difficulty recalling what was said or seen. Many times as a language teacher, we struggle to create activities that capture all three of these learning styles. Well, struggle no more! With the Creation of Art technique, (COA) all three learning styles are incorporated into the activities and students make the learning experience meaningful by making it **PERSONAL**. The **CREATION** of their own artwork and the use of that work in classroom activities puts the learning in context and provides the learner an excellent chance of grasping the material, and enhancing their memory of it.

Also, a **BONUS** for teachers is the fact that the technique takes almost **NO PREPARATION TIME** on the part of the teacher. The students do the preparation by doing the artwork, and learn more in the process. Teachers only need to follow the simple directions given for each activity.

How Does it Work?

1) Students are instructed at the beginning of the year (or semester) to come to class with their regular classroom supplies (book, pen, notebook, etc…) and also with specific art supplies. The teacher can decide what media is feasible for students to use according to the classroom that is available. For example, if students have access to an art room without carpet and with a sink, any form of media would be acceptable. If teachers need to use a regular classroom, teachers need to suggest only crayons, pastels, markers, colored pencils, etc… as long as it is not paint. It is also

---

** http://www.usd.edu/trio/tut/ts/styleres.html/ adapted from Instructor Magazine, 8-89

necessary that they have color. It is suggested that students should start with crayons or markers for the first few activities, until they become comfortable with the use of art in the language learning environment, and then if possible, teachers can switch to paint. Watercolors would be an excellent choice as they are extremely economical, and easy to carry. In some of the activities other types of special materials are suggested (such as clay or play-dough, and large poster boards) and teachers may choose whether or not they want to use those materials. If they do, it is advisable to have students buy their own supplies ahead of time, or have students pay a fee at the beginning of class and have the teacher use this money to buy the supplies. If teachers are working with students with limited funds, teachers can have students use their regular notebook paper, and students can be required to use only one low-cost form of media (such as crayons or colored pencils) and they can share them among 3-4 students in the class.

2) Students are told that one of the techniques that will be used in the class is the COA (Creation of Art) technique. Teachers inform students that the technique will be used for one-two activities per class (depending on the length of the class) and will be only one of many different techniques used during the course. The goal of the technique is to enhance memory and increase understanding of concepts by utilizing as many senses as possible while they learn and by making the learning personal. Students will be asked to create various types of artwork during the course, and they will use their creations to produce and understand the target language. It is important that students know right away that this technique **DOES NOT TEACH ART** and students will **NOT** be graded on their art creations. The art will merely be a MEANS through which they will facilitate their language learning.

3) Teachers should choose the first activity to be one in which the art skill is minimal (such as the color/animal activity) so that students will not feel intimidated or embarrassed by their artwork. More difficult art activities can be done later on in the course when students are accustomed to the whole process..

4) It is very important that students follow these **GUIDELINES** for the creation of each work of art.

- Students must know the goal of the activity (teachers need to inform students, eg… we will be working on the present perfect)
- As they draw, students must **SAY OUT LOUD** or REPEAT to themselves, what they are drawing in the target language (ex… flower, flower, I am drawing a flower). This will help bring together all the senses used so they are using their body (drawing), speaking (repetition), listening (to themselves) and seeing (looking at what they are drawing) throughout the whole exercise.
- All activities centered around the COA must be done **ENTIRELY** in the target language. Teachers must give instructions in the target language, and students must interact with each other only in the target language.

It might be helpful for teachers to distribute a list of suggested conversation phrases for art activities so that students won't be tempted to use their native language while working on their art projects. Here is a sample list of some possible suggested phrases;

Helpful Conversation Tips for Classroom Art Activities:

- Could I borrow your: pen, pencil, crayon, marker, paint, paper?
- I like your: drawing, picture, painting.
- What do we need to do?
- How much time do we have?
- Yours is: funny, cute, interesting, nice, hilarious, silly, excellent.
- Mine is … .
- I don't understand what is happening in your picture.
- Could you explain to me what is in your drawing/painting?
- I need more: time, paper, crayons.
- Do we need to write anything on the drawing/ painting?
- I like how you: drew that, put that, labeled that.

Note:
- These activities are aimed at English as a Second Language classrooms, but can be easily adapted to the teaching of **ANY LANGUAGE,** not just English.
- Most of the activities in the book **OVERLAP SEVERAL SKILLS** (such

as the vocabulary activities involve writing and speaking and listening) but they are listed under a specific category that the teacher might need to emphasize.
- In order to accommodate all the needs of a language class, this technique should not be used for the entire class period, but it is suggested that teachers use one to two activities per week depending on the length of the class.
- Students should be instructed that they will have only limited time to complete each picture, and if they so desire, they can beautify or add more detail to their artwork at home. They must be expeditious in their drawings in order to make the class time productive.
- Depending on the curriculum load for the course, teachers might want to assign some of the artwork as homework, and have students come with their artwork the next day, ready for the activity.
- The activities are marked according to level, (beginning, intermediate, and advanced) and although they are aimed at university/community college level, they can be adapted to all age levels and types of students.
- Students that feel intimidated by art should be told that bad art makes for a better language experience (there will be a need for more clarification and more questions) as well as more fun, and that no one is there to judge their artwork.
- Teachers of students with limited resources may not want to ask their students to buy their own art supplies. In this case, there are several options.

1) Teachers may choose to work together with art teachers at the institution they are working with. Many art teachers are very happy to be a part of the integration of art into language classes. They may have access to cheap art supplies, or may have extra materials that would have otherwise been discarded that they could provide teachers with.
2) Students could pool together and share art supplies among a group. In this case it is recommended that the teacher keep a special box with the art supplies in it in the classroom.
3) Teachers may choose to visit art stores and places such as wallpaper stores or craft stores and ask if they have leftover pieces of fabric, framing poster paper, or other materials that might come in handy.
4) Teachers can ask each student to bring in one magazine to keep in the classroom for collages. This magazine supply will be built on with each group of students the teacher has.

Helpful Art Tips for Classroom Art Activities:

For those teachers who are interested in art, and want to improve their own artwork, or teachers who have students that inquire about improving their art technique, there are many different websites that offer quick tips for the beginning artists. Some recommended ones are; www.artsillustration.com, www.delusionstudio.com, and www.drawright.com. If interested, teachers can try to incorporate some of these tips into their first few art activities to help students become more comfortable with their drawing, or help students interested in the art aspect as well as learning the language, improve in both areas. If teachers choose to help students with the art aspect by using these tips, it is important that teachers do this in the TARGET LANGUAGE so that students are learning the appropriate vocabulary in the target language (in this case, English) as well as art skills. It should also be emphasized to other students that the art aspect is just a bonus to this language technique, and it is the language learning that is the real focus, therefore, students should not be concerned with the quality of their artwork, but with their language learning.

How to Use This Book

Each chapter in the book addresses a different skill. The chapters are VOCABULARY, READING, WRITING, GRAMMAR, SPEAKING, and LISTENING. Since many of the activities overlap skills (such as many speaking activities involve listening and writing as well as reading), teachers can decide which skill they want to emphasize that day, and choose an activity accordingly. Teachers should use this book to build on and review concepts that have been taught briefly or extensively. Teachers need only to look up in the TABLE of CONTENTS what they are working on, and then find the page number of the activity for that concept.

Example:
1) A teacher is reviewing vocabulary for body parts.
2) She/he looks up "body parts" in the table of contents, and finds activity 1.9. Body Parts.
3) Teacher finds the correct page and reads over the instructions.
4) Most activities require no special materials on the part of the teacher, but if there are special materials needed (such as poster paper for a mural), they will be listed at the beginning of the activity.

Note:
1) When adapting activities for younger students, teachers must take into account whether students can read or write, and adapt or change the activity to fit students at this level.
2) For large classrooms difficult to manage, teachers should stick to activities that don't need a lot of movement or change the activity so students will not need to move around as much.
3) When choosing an activity, teachers should read over the VARIATIONS listed at the bottom of many of the activities. The VARIATIONS often provide a suitable adaptation for different class types.

Chapter One

Vocabulary Activities

Introduction

Like all activities in this book, the vocabulary activities should be executed AFTER the words or grammatical concepts (some are incorporated into the vocabulary activities) have already been introduced. The activities should facilitate memory and understanding of the concepts, but not be the first introduction to the concepts. It is recommended that teachers assign students to study the vocabulary ahead of time (with the exception of very young students) and then go over the words for meaning and pronunciation before beginning the COA activities. Although the activities in this section are targeting a specific vocabulary, many of them can be easily adapted to fit any vocabulary given at any level. For example, the clothing activity (making ads for an assigned piece of clothing) could be used for any object vocabulary such as household appliances, cars, vacation locations, etc…) or the food activity (drawing your favorite meal) could be applied to any hobby or class or country. Teachers may want to incorporate other grammatical structures or communicative vocabulary into any of the activities according to what students have already learned. For example, when students are learning colors or classroom objects, their vocabulary and grammar is quite limited, so teachers may want to stick to the repetition phrases given, and the set questions. If teachers choose to use Activity 1.1 for more advanced vocabulary such as talking about their jobs or talking about relationships or more advanced adjectives, they would be able to add more complex questions and encourage more open conversations as people share their artwork.

It is important to remember that all of the COA activities must be done completely in the target language, and students must be given the GOAL, and a REPETITION PHRASE to be saying or thinking while they are creating their artwork.

1.1 Colors/Animals/Classroom Objects

Level: Beginning- Intermediate

Goal: Review of vocabulary taught (this could be colors and animals or colors and classroom objects, or for more advanced students, adjectives describing animals or vocabulary to discuss jobs, or vocabulary dealing with relationships, etc.). OPTIONAL: To review questions with the verb "to be", negatives and possessive adjectives.

Note: For this description of the activity, colors and classroom objects will be used. If teachers decided to use this activity with more advanced vocabulary, they could adapt the questions and repetition phrases to fit that vocabulary.

Repetition Phrase: The _____ is _____. (ex: *The backpack is yellow.*) Or if students have learned possessive pronouns; *My pencil is brown.* (If doing animals, *My dog is brown.* Or if they have learned the verb "have", *"I have a brown dog." "I have a red book."* The possibilities for repetition phrases are many, and depend on what students have previously learned.

Procedure:
1) The teacher assigns each student a previously learned vocabulary word and a color.

2) Students must draw their word (such as *book*) and color or paint it any color they wish.
3) Students must say "The _____ is _____." (ex: The chair is beige.) while they are drawing it.
4) Students are instructed to get up with their drawing/ painting and walk around and find a partner.
5) Once they have found a partner, Student A says 1) "The _____ is _____." taking a guess at what the student drew and what color it is. 2) For more advanced students have them practice forming sentences such as "Is that a *blue book* ? If using 2), teachers need to mingle around the room to check for the correct use of the verb "to be" in questions.
6) Student B answers "Yes, my _____ is _____." Or "No, my _____ is not brown." Or "No, it is not a _____ _____." This part then enforces the use of negatives.
7) More advanced students can ask more complex questions of their own choice about the drawings.
8) Students now find a new partner and repeat steps 5 and 6.
9) Students continue until the teacher says time is up.

Variations:
1) As discussed earlier, vocabulary and questions/ repetition phrases can be changed to fit more advanced levels.
2) Students can work in groups of four and learn all the objects and colors in their group. In plenary, one student at a time can stand up and show their drawing to the class and say "My _____ is _____." or whatever their repetition phrase is.
3) After students have presented their drawings, the teacher can ask questions to the class as a whole. Ex: Who has a brown bear? OR Whose backpack is red?

1.2 Time

Level: Beginning-intermediate

Goal: Learn to tell time in the target language, incorporate use of the simple present + adverbs of frequency (usually, never, always, rarely, often, sometimes)

Repetition Phrases:
- A) It is _____ o'clock.
- B) At _____ I _____ (usually, often, etc..) _____. (eat dinner, do my homework, etc…) This is whatever they drew in the picture.

Procedure:
1) Teacher instructs students to draw a small clock in the top left-hand corner (dry media is suggested for this activity) and put a time on it. Students should say "It is _____ o'clock." while they are drawing.
2) Teacher writes the adverbs of frequency on the board and discusses meaning.
3) Students choose a regular activity that they do and draw it in the center of the paper. They must say "At _____ I _____ _____." (ex: At 5 o'clock I eat dinner.) while they are drawing.
4) Teacher instructs students to walk around the room with their drawings, and find a partner. Student A looks at Student B's picture and says "At _____ you _____ _____. (according to the clock time on the drawing, and according to what the student has drawn)
5) When Student A has completed Step 4, Student B completes Step 4 looking at Student A's drawing.
6) When Student B has finished, students move on to find another partner until thethe teacher says time is up.
7) In plenary, the teacher calls on several students to share their drawings and say repetition phrases.

1.3 Family

Level: Beginning

Goal: To review the names of family members, use the simple present, form questions, review prepositions of location

Repetition Phrases: This is my _____. (insert family member title such as aunt, uncle, cousin, etc…) OR My (aunt, uncle, sister, etc…) is _____ (-ing form of verb).

Procedure:

Special Materials: Students need to bring magazines, glue, scissors, extra copies or printouts of family photos, and any particular materials they want to use to make a collage of their families.

1) Teacher puts up family member names (such as aunt, uncle, sister, etc...) on the overhead or computer for students to look at.
2) Students are asked to take out their family photos (if they have forgotten them or have none, they will have to draw them or use pictures of other people from a magazine) and collage materials.
3) Teacher tells students they are to make a collage showing their family members including in-laws, step-brothers, and any extended family members, doing something together.
4) As students glue their family members onto the paper, they need to say the repetition phrase (This is my _____.) For more advanced students, they may say "My aunt is _____." using the present progressive.
5) After students have completed their collages they need to get up and find a partner.
6) The teacher should then ask students what kinds of questions could they ask about each other's family members. The teacher needs to make sure students are forming the questions correctly. The teacher then writes these questions down on the board, correcting grammar mistakes as they appear.

Possible questions:

- *Where is your sister?*
- *Where is your mother?*
- *Who is that?*
- *What is your sister doing?*
- *What is your sister's name?*
- *Is this everyone in your family?*

7) Student A asks Student B some of the questions on the board, or forms new questions about Student B's collage.
8) When Student A has completed step 7, Student B asks Student A the questions.
9) When Student B has completed step 7, he/she finds a new partner and completes steps 1-8.

10) Students continue the activity until time is up.
11) In plenary, the teacher asks students to write on the board any new questions they came up with. Students and teacher correct the questions for grammatical errors, and the teacher calls on several people to answer them.

Variation: If time is limited, have students make the collage as homework, making sure they know the repetition phrase and the goals. Have students complete the procedure in class starting with step 5.

1.4 Days of the Week

Level: Beginning

Goal: To review the days of the week and practice use of the simple present

Repetition Phrases: On Mondays I _____. On Tuesdays I _____.
(the day depends on which day they are assigned by the teacher)

NOTE: Students should not use this activity until they are familiar with some common verbs such as eat, study, swim, walk, work, etc...

Procedure:
1) Teacher reviews days of the week orally with the students.
2) Students are instructed to draw one thing they do on one day of the week. Paper large enough to see from a distance is recommended for this activity. Teachers should assign several students (depending on the number of students) one day so that every day is represented by several people.
3) Students repeat the correct repetition phrase as they draw, and write the repetition phrase on the bottom of the paper.
4) Teacher circulates the room and writes down some of the more common verbs she sees students using. Teacher also checks for correct use of simple present.
5) When students have finished drawing, the teacher asks all students to stand. The teacher writes the days of the week on the board in columns.
6) Teacher asks "Who eats out on Fridays?" "Who plays soccer on Sundays?" etc... Teacher has students who raise their hands come to the front of the

room and stand holding up their drawing, under the day of the week of their activity that is written on the board.
7) The teacher then asks the remaining students "Who plays soccer on Sundays?" etc… Students must find the students under the correct day and answer the question. If the students get the answer correct, the student who the question was about holds up his/her drawing to show the activity with the repetition phrase next to it.

Variation:
1) Students complete steps 1-3.
2) Students divide into pairs and Student A asks "What do you do on _____?"(insert day of the week).
3) Student B answers the question and asks partner the same question.
4) Students continue steps 2 and 3 with a new partner.
5) Students continue until time is up.

1.5 Feelings

Level: Beginning –advanced

Goal: Review adjectives describing feelings, review verbs in the simple present

Repetition Phrase: When _____, I feel _____. **Ex:** When my car breaks down, I feel frustrated.

Procedure:
1) Teacher assigns students to study the adjectives describing feelings the day before this activity is planned. The level of the activity depends on the level of the adjectives chosen for the activity. For beginners, adjectives like happy, sad, or angry, should be used. For intermediate – advanced students, adjectives such as jealous, loquacious, miserable, frustrated, etc…are recommended.
2) Teacher assigns each student an adjective from the list, and tells students to draw (or paint) something happening that makes them feel that way.
3) While students are drawing (or painting), they should be saying aloud the repetition phrase "When _____, I feel _____." Students should also write the repetition phrase on the back of the drawing, or if they painted, in very small letters in the bottom right-hand corner of the drawing.

4) Teacher should be circulating at this time, to be sure students are repeating the phrase correctly, and are using the correct verbs.
5) When students have finished their drawings, the teacher asks them to form two lines facing each other, in front of the room. Each student is the partner of the student he/she is facing.
6) Student A tries to guess what Student B's repetition phrase (and simultaneously, the feeling they were assigned) is. Student A continues to guess several times or until they get it right.
7) Student A repeats Student B's repetition phrase.
8) Student B completes steps 6 and 7 for Student A's artwork.
9) The student at the very left of the line facing the board goes to the end of the line so he/she is now on the right side of the line, and all the students in his/her line move down one person, so they all have a new partner.
10) Repeat steps 6-9 until students in one line have guessed the repetition phrases of all students in the line facing them.

1.6 Describing People

Level: Beginning-advanced

Goal: Review adjectives describing people (both physical qualities and personality traits).

Repetition Phrase: "She/he is _____, _____, and _____."

Special Materials: Clay, or play-dough is recommended for this activity. Clay is much better, but also more expensive. It is recommended that teachers charge a small fee for each student, and buy 2 packs of no-bake clay (any craft store will have it) for about $16, or 2 packs of play-dough for about $3. If teachers prefer, they can have students buy a small pack of clay or play-dough as part of their materials for the class, at the beginning of the semester. Teachers must remind students to save their sculptures (along with all their artwork) if teachers wish to use the Art Show activity at the end of the course.

Procedure:
1) Teacher reviews words used to describe people physically (tall, blond, handsome) and also words used to describe personality traits (energetic, lazy, funny).

2) Teacher models to students by writing three sentences on the board using three of the adjectives from the list.

   Example: He has a beautiful voice.
             He is very large.
             He sings opera.

   Students must try to guess who it is (Answer = Luciano Pavarotti). When students have guessed correctly, teacher shows them his/her sculpture of Luciano Pavarotti. Teachers will want to use their own example choosing someone popular among the students, or famous at the time of the activity.
3) Students are directed to do the same thing the teacher modeled, and make a famous person (or animal or object) out of clay or play-dough and write three clues using adjectives from the list reviewed at the beginning of class.
4) Students need to say their clues aloud as they make the person, and the teacher should go around the room checking their work, and answering questions.
5) After steps 3-4 are completed, teacher divides students into groups of four.
6) Students read their clues aloud, one by one, and the other students from the group try to guess the person they made. When they have guessed correctly, the student whose person they were guessing holds up the sculpture they made for the students to see.
7) When all students in the group have completed step 6, they choose the student with the most difficult person to guess, to present to the class.
8) The chosen students come to the front of the class and read (one at a time) their clues for the whole class to guess.

Variation:
1) Students are assigned to make the sculptures at home the day before the activity.
2) Students bring their sculptures and sentences to class, and complete steps 5-8.

1.7 Occupations

Level: Beginning-Intermediate

Goal: To review the vocabulary for occupations, and use them in context

Repetition Phrase: My dream is to be _____. (**an** engineer, a carpenter, etc..)

Procedure:
1) Students are divided into groups of four and told to brainstorm all the occupations they have learned so far, and find the words for occupations they want to learn. Students should make sure occupations they would like to have or already have are on the list.
2) Students are told to choose which job would be their dream job – a job they would love to have. Students then draw the job (dry media is suggested for this activity) and say aloud the repetition phrase as they draw.
3) Students should write their repetition phrase at the bottom of the drawing.
4) When students have completed step 3, they must turn over their drawing and write 3-5 clues about their occupation.

   Example: This person makes cakes.
   This person makes pies.
   This person works in a bakery.
   This person uses an oven.
   Who is it?
      (Answer: Baker)

5) When students have completed step 4, they must get up and walk around the room looking for a partner.
6) Student A reads his/her clues to her partner (make sure Student A has another book or notebook underneath the paper he/she is reading, so Student B can't see the answer on the back) and Student B tries to guess what Student A's dream job is.
7) When Student B has guessed correctly, Student A shows Student B the answer (and drawing) on the other side of the paper. Student B then reads his/her clues and Student A tries to guess his/her dream job.
8) When Student B has completed step 7, both students look for a new partner.
9) Students continue guessing the other students' dream jobs until teacher calls time.
10) In plenary, teacher gives clues about the students' dream jobs.

    Example: Whose dream job involves cutting trees?
    Who must learn about marine biology to have this occupation?

Chapter 1: Vocabulary Activities   11

Students must recognize that the teacher is calling on their occupation, and stand holding up their artwork so the other students can see the answer.

Variation:
Teachers may choose to have students make their worker out of clay or playdough instead of drawing them.

1.8 Food

Level: Beginning-intermediate

Goal: Speaking, review of food vocabulary

Repetition Phrase:
    For breakfast, we eat_____.
    For lunch, we eat _____.
    For dinner, we eat _____.
    For a snack, we eat _____.

Special Materials: Magazines, scissors, glue

Procedure:
1) Students find foods they like in magazines.
2) Students are divided into groups of three or four students.
3) Together, students must divide all the food cut out from all group members into breakfast, lunch, dinner, and snacks.
4) Each student is assigned to do one meal.
5) Students paste all of their meal items on one page, so each group member is putting together one page.
6) While putting together the page, each student should be saying their repetition phrase, and writing the food item's name next to the food item.
7) When students have completed step 6, the teacher will call on each group to present their meals at the front of the class. Each person in each group should present their meal (saying the name for each food item as they point to it) separately.

Variations:
1) Students can do this activity at home, and present all of their meals in their group of 3 or 4 students.
2) Students can work in groups and draw or paint their favorite meals to present.
3) Each group can be assigned one meal, and each person in each group can draw (or find) one food item from that meal.
4) Students can be divided into groups and assigned one meal. Each student in each group must BRING to class (the next day) that actual food item for all class members to eat. Students must label their food item correctly and all students should present the food items and their names (in the target language of course) before eating.
5) For ADVANCED students, have students look up a recipe on the internet in the target language. Teachers may need to guide students on how to search on the internet for recipes in the target language. Students must print out the recipe and illustrate it. Students must then follow the directions in the target language to make the recipe, and say aloud the instructions as they perform them (such as pour in 2 cups of flour, mix all ingredients together). Students take their food to class the following day. In class, students paste their recipe and picture on the actual food item, and each student presents the food item they made before students eat.

* For Variation 5, teachers will want to give students a list of cooking terminology in the target language (such as heat, simmer, mix, fold, cups, teaspoons, etc...)

1.9 Body Parts

Level: Beginning -intermediate

Goal: To review the vocabulary for body parts, writing

Repetition Phrase: These are the directions students give to draw the body parts.

Special Materials: Teacher or students need to bring one large piece of paper (very light cheap material), large enough to lie on. There should be one piece of paper for every two students. Teachers can buy a large roll at any art store, or see if there are any extra rolls in the art department at the school they are teaching at. Students need to have markers as well.

Procedure:
1) Teacher reviews names of body parts with students, making them touch the body part as they say it.
2) Students are divided into pairs.
3) Student A lies down on his/her paper, and Student B traces his/her body shape onto the paper.
4) Student B dictates a body part and color to Student A, and Student A colors it onto the traced body.

    Example: "Draw a blue mouth." "Draw red pants on the legs." "Draw a gold bracelet on the wrist." More advanced students can be asked to add more adjectives and more complex body parts.

5) When Student A has dictated for 5 minutes, Student A now tells Student B what to draw.
6) Teacher calls time and students must hang up their bodies around the room.
7) Teacher explains that this is a race. When she/ he calls time, students must run up (with their partner) and try to label as many parts as possible.
8) When time is up, teacher explains that students will get one point for each correctly spelled body part in the correct place.
9) Teacher goes to each body and reads aloud each body part labeled. Students repeat after the teacher. Teacher makes corrections when needed and does not give points for incorrectly spelled body parts.
10) When the counting is done, the team with the most points wins.
11) Students may take their bodies home.

1.10 Sports

Level: Beginning- Intermediate

Goal: Speaking, to review sports' vocabulary, seasons, and CAN /CANNOT

Repetition Phrase:
In the summer, you can _____.
In the fall, you cannot _____.
In the spring, you can _____.
In the winter, you cannot _____.

Procedure:
1) Teacher asks students to name the four seasons.
2) Teacher writes the seasons on the board. Under each season she/he writes CAN in one column and CANNOT in the other.
3) Students are divided into groups to review sports vocabulary.
4) Each group is assigned one season.
5) Several people in each group must draw (dry media is suggested) a sport that CAN be done during that season, and several people must draw a sport that CANNOT be done during that season.
6) While drawing, students must repeat the name of the season they were assigned with the repetition phrase (use CAN or CANNOT depending on what they were assigned by the group).
7) When time is up, students must attach (blue poster putty works well) their sport under the appropriate season and CAN or CANNOT column.
8) In plenary, teacher asks questions about each sport and calls on each student to answer. EXAMPLE QUESTIONS: "Which sports can we play in the fall and winter, but not in the summer or spring?" "Which sports can be played only in the summer?"

Variation:
1) Students complete steps 1-6.
2) Students work with a partner from a different group, and present their drawings while saying their repetition phrases to each other.
3) Instead of drawing, students can cut out pictures from magazines, or if students have access, they can use the internet and print out pictures. If necessary, this can be done as homework and students can bring the pictures to class the next day to use for the activity.

1.11 Weather/Months

Level: Beginning – Intermediate

Goal: To review weather vocabulary and months of the year.

Repetition Phrase: It's _____ (cloudy, sunny, snowing, raining, etc.)

Procedure:
1) Teacher goes over weather vocabulary with students.
2) Teacher assigns each student a weather word (cloudy, sunny, humid, etc.)
3) Students must draw or paint their weather word.
4) While drawing/painting, students must repeat the repetition phrase according to the word they were assigned, and write it at the bottom of the paper.
5) When students have completed their artwork, in plenary, the teacher asks students to brainstorm cities around the world.
6) Teacher calls on twelve students (each city will have one month written under it) to tell her/him a city and writes these cities up on the board as they are dictated to her/him.
7) Teacher asks for a volunteer to write one month under each city.
8) The volunteer writes the months on the board as students say them.
9) Teacher asks students to divide into groups of 3-4 students and brainstorm 10 questions. Each question must contain a weather word, a city, and a month.

    Example: What's the weather like in Chicago in May? How's the weather in Florida in September?

10) After students have completed step 9, each group must pick a questioner.
11) The questioners from each group take turns asking the rest of the class the questions their group wrote.
12) After each question is asked, the students who drew the weather that answers the questions (Example: What's the weather like in Chicago in May?) — all students with "It's cold." "It's snowy." "It's icy," stand up. There may be some disagreements as to the correct answer. Teacher can turn to the internet and look up the weather for each city, and discuss the correct answer with students if needed.
13) Students continue step 12 until all questioners have asked all their questions or time is up.

Variation 1:
1) Students complete steps 1-4.
2) Students think of their own questions about their own picture regarding the weather.
3) Students work in pairs.
4) Student A shows Student B his/her picture, and asks the questions regarding the weather. EX: What's the weather like in this picture?
5) When Student A has completed step 4, Student B completes step 4.
6) After completing step 5, students find another partner and repeat steps 4 and 5.
7) Students continue with new partners until teacher calls time.

Variation 2:
1) Students complete steps 1-6.
2) Students write a question including the weather, month, and city with the answer being their repetition phrase (It's _____.)
3) Students work in pairs.
4) Student A asks Student B his/her question, and when the student answers, Student A shows Student B the drawing with the picture and correct answer written on the bottom.
5) Repeat step 4 with Student B asking the question.
6) Continue steps 3-5 finding new partners each time, until teacher calls time.

1.12 Clothing

Level: Intermediate-Advanced

Goal: To review present simple verbs, imperatives, colors, and clothing vocabulary.

Repetition Phrase: This is a black shirt (will vary according to clothing and color assigned).

Special Materials: Scissors

Procedure:
1) Students review the clothing vocabulary with the teacher.

2) Teacher assigns each student a type of clothing (shoes, scarf, skirt, etc...) and a color.
3) Each student must draw a quick picture of the clothing item in the proper color and cut it out. Students must repeat the repetition phrase while drawing.
4) Students are divided into groups of 3-4 and given three choices.

   a) Create a commercial for the clothing each student in the group has drawn.
   b) Role-play a scene in a clothing store using the clothing drawings created in class.
   c) Create a fashion show using the drawings the students have created in some way to present the clothing.

5) Teacher circulates to answer questions students have on vocabulary, and make sure students are incorporating the use of imperatives into their activities.

   Example: a) Come quick! All our sweaters are 50% off. Buy now!
             b) Try it on! Please get me a pair in size 10.
             c) Everyone look carefully. These new fall fashions will soon be all the rage in your city. Order now!

6) Students work on their group projects in class and present them at the end of class, OR they work on them separately and present them at a later date.

1.13 City Locations

Level: Beginning

Goal: To practice location vocabulary and giving and following directions for locations.

Repetition Phrase: You are at the post office and you want to go to the bank. To arrive at the bank, go straight, turn right on Dodge Street, and go straight. The bank is on your left. (Students think of a destination starting from the building they drew on the mural and practice saying how to get there)

Special Materials: Large paper for the class to make a mural.

Procedure:
1) Teacher asks students to turn to the page in the book that shows locations of buildings (like post office, bank, museum, etc...) or teacher supplies students with a handout with the target vocabulary listed and reviews with students the vocabulary and basic direction vocabulary (straight, left, right, south, east, turn, go, past, blocks, etc...).
2) Teacher (or a volunteer student) draws a simple map of about five streets on the mural. The map should be of streets only, and should be large enough for students to draw buildings on both sides of each street. Students must discuss names for each street and label them.
3) Teacher assigns each student one building (like post office, bank, etc...) to draw on the side of any of the streets. Students must begin thinking of their repetition phrases and practice these while drawing.
4) After all students have drawn their buildings on the map, each student writes down their destination questions starting with the building they drew (see repetition phrases).
5) Teacher posts up the mural so all students can see it.
6) Students are divided into pairs, and Student A reads his/her repetition phrase and Student B must answer it, looking at the mural as a guide.
7) When Student B has answered Student A's question, Student B now reads his/her question and Student A answers it.
8) When teacher calls time, students exchange partners.
9) Students complete Steps 6 and 7 with new partners.
10) Continue until time is up, or all students have completed Steps 6 and 7 with all other students.
11) In plenary, teacher calls on students with a few questions (Example: If I am at the library, how do I get to the town hall?)

Variations:
1) Students are divided into groups and each group chooses its own area to draw a map of, and students in the group divide up the area and illustrate the various landmarks. Each group then chooses a representative to present their maps to the class and describe in detail the location of each landmark.
2) Students can do the group work (including the illustrations) as homework, and present several sample dialogs giving and following directions to the class the next day based on their maps.

1.14 Dance Line

Level: Intermediate-Advanced

Goal: To review nature vocabulary in context, adjectives, speaking in general. This activity can be adapted easily for any vocabulary list the teacher wants to review or reinforce.

Repetition Phrase: Will vary depending on the words used in the pictures.

Procedure:
1) Teacher reviews with students nature vocabulary words (such as mountain, lake, valley, river, tree, farm, etc...) and checks for understanding.
2) Each student is assigned three random nature words and told to use those words in a sentence. Advanced students are encouraged to make complex sentences using creative adjectives
3) Students write the sentence (this is their repetition phrase)at the bottom of the paper.
4) Students illustrate their sentence (Example sentence: The beautiful *river* runs through the lush *valley* and supplies the *village* people with water. Words used: river, valley, village). Students repeat the repetition phrase while painting. Wet media is recommended.
5) When students have completed their paintings, the class is divided into two groups. The students in Group A must stand in various places around the room, holding up their paintings or laying them out on the desk in front of them if they are not yet dry.
6) If students don't understand the picture or vocabulary, they may ask Group A students to clarify or explain.
7) During this interaction time, the teacher turns on music in the target language to indicate that students in Group B must move down the line and repeat step 6 listening to the next student from Group A's repetition phrase.
8) Each time students move from one person to the next (with music on), they must dance to their next spot. Teacher turns off or pauses music when students are reading their repetition phrases. When teacher turns on music, students in Group B only move to the next person.
9) When all students in Group B have seen all students' artwork from Group A, students from Group A put down their artwork, and students from Group B get their artwork, and stand in a line around the room ready to complete steps 6-8, showing their artwork and repeating their repetition phrases.

10) Continue until all students from Group A have seen all of Group B's artwork.

1.15 Transportation

Level: Beginning- Intermediate

Goal: To review transportation words in context

Repetition Phrase: It is _____, _____, and. It can be used to _____. You can travel _____ with it.

> Example: It is large, yellow, and long. It can be used to <u>carry 20-50 children to school</u>. You can travel <u>on land</u> with it.

Procedure:
1) Teacher assigns students to study the transportation words at home, the day before this activity.
2) Students are assigned one word from the list of transportation words, and asked to illustrate their word in some kind of appropriate context (EX: a bus taking people from the city to the country, or a boat, taking fishermen out to sea).
3) While drawing, students should be saying the repetition phrases aloud to practice.
4) After the drawing is complete, students turn over the paper and write the repetition phrase on the back of their paper.
5) Students grab a book to put under their drawing and mingle around the room from partner to partner completing steps 6-8.
6) In pairs, Student A reads their clues to Student B careful not to let Student B see their drawing on the other side. Student B tries to guess the transportation vehicle from listening to the clues.
7) When Student B guesses correctly, Student A turns over the paper and lets Student B see the illustration. Student B must say aloud (from memory) Student A's repetition phrases that go along with Student A's illustration.
8) Students repeat steps 6 and 7 with Student B's phrases and illustration, and Student A guessing.

Chapter 1: Vocabulary Activities   21

9) Continue until time is up, or all students have seen each other's illustrations.

Variation:
1) Students make a mural with their transportation vehicles and label each vehicle. The mural is displayed at the front of the room. This is the illustration at the beginning of this chapter.
2) Each student writes clues for their vehicle and keeps them.
3) The teacher calls on several students to read their clues to the class and have students guess the vehicle. Students refer to the mural to help them choose.

1.16 Human Art Bingo

Level: Beginning - Advanced

Goal: General vocabulary review (best with words that are easily illustrated)

Repetition Phrase: This is a _____. OR Use the vocabulary word in a sentence.

Procedure:
1) Teacher chooses any list of easily illustratable words to review. This is also an excellent game for end of the semester or year review.
2) Each student is assigned one word from the list to illustrate. Students repeat the repetition phrase while drawing.
3) Teacher tells the students that the class is a human bingo card. Each student represents a square. When the teacher calls the vocabulary item, the student with that picture must stand up and use the word in a sentence correctly. This cannot be the repetition phrase. If the student completes the sentence correctly, the student may remain standing. If the student does not complete the sentence correctly, the student must sit down. If a student is the last person in the row to stand up, he/she yells "Bingo". In order for the row to win, all students in the row must repeat their sentences using the bingo words correctly.
4) If students in the row do not say their sentences correctly, they must sit down and the class must start over. When starting over, all students must

move to a different seat and get a different word, OR just get a different word but not move seats.

5) If students win, they should be rewarded with bonus points for the test, or candy, or a free homework assignment – whatever the teacher knows would be good motivation for students to win. If time is up and the students have not won, the teacher can give a quiz on the vocabulary words the next day, or assign extra homework (this will be good motivation for students to play and win).

Variation:
- If there are fewer than 8 students, game does not work well. In this case, the same activity could be used to play "Human Tic-Tac-Toe" and have two teams against each other.
- For fewer than 25 students (but more than 8) group students according to these numbers;

    20 = 4 rows of 5
    18 = 3 rows of 5, 1 row of 3
    16 = 4 rows of 4
    12 = 3 rows of 4
    10 = 2 rows of 3, 1 row of 4
    8 = 2 rows of 3, 1 row of 2

    * for odd numbers, have one extra in one of the rows

1.17 Relay

Level: Beginning- Advanced

Goal: To review any vocabulary list or to review vocabulary for an exam (vocabulary that is easy to illustrate works best). This is also a good writing activity.

Repetition Phrase: This is a _____. OR For advanced students, use the vocabulary word in a sentence.

Chapter 1: Vocabulary Activities

Procedure:
1) Teacher provides students with a list of vocabulary words to review. Teacher goes over the words orally for pronunciation purposes.
2) Each student is assigned one word from the list to illustrate on a large piece of paper. Beginning students must write the word on the back of the picture, and repeat "This is a _____", while drawing. More advanced students must use the word in a sentence as their repetition phrase, and write that sentence on the back of the picture.
3) After students have illustrated their words, they are divided into teams.
4) The teacher collects all the illustrations and asks one member from each team to go to the board.
5) The teacher holds up a picture of the word, and the students must write the name of the word on the board. If no students can figure out what the word is by looking at the picture, the teacher must say the sentence written on the back or make up her own sentence (saying BLANK where the word in the illustration is) and students try to guess the word from the sentence.
6) The first person to get the correct answer and say the name of the word correctly to the teacher, gets a point.
7) Students take turns going to the board until all words have been written on the board once.

1.18 Swat the Flies

Level: Beginning – Advanced

Goal: General review of vocabulary, writing

Repetition Phrase: This is a _____.

Special Materials: *One fly-swatter per team. Fly swatters may be brought by students or purchased by the teacher for around 50 cents each at any supermarket.

Procedure:
1) Students are given a list of vocabulary words to review in groups.

---

* Optional: If the blackboard is too small, or there are not enough pens, teachers can bring in a giant piece of poster paper for students to use as a mural.

2) When students have studied the vocabulary words for several minutes, the teacher assigns each student one word.
3) Students must go to the board OR the mural paper, and illustrate their word. They must repeat the repetition phrase as they draw.
4) When students have finished their drawings the mural is posted on the wall (if using the blackboard, students will simply refer to the blackboard).
5) Students are divided into teams and each team receives a fly swatter.
6) Each team sends one member of the team to the board or mural with a pen or chalk.
7) When the teacher calls out a word from the list (or for more advanced students, when the teacher reads a sentence for the students to guess a word to complete) the students look for the picture of the word on the mural or board, and must swat that word with their fly-swatter.
8) The team that swats the correct word first, must write the word next to its picture correctly. If the team member does these two things correctly FIRST, their team gets a point. If the team member swats the word but does not write it correctly, the team members of the other teams get a chance to write the word correctly and whoever writes it correctly first, gets the point.

Variation:
1) Teachers can use this activity to review verbs in the present tense as well by having students illustrate the subject (I, you, he/she, etc…) and the verb (by showing what the subject is doing).
2) Students then use the subject and verb in a sentence for their repetition phrase, and complete steps 3-7 using their verb illustrations. The teacher then calls out the verb with the subject in the illustration, and students must swat the verb and use the verb in a sentence with its subject. This variation can also be applied to activity 1.17 (Relay)

References

Woodward, S. (1997). *Fun With Grammar; Communicative Activities for the Azar Grammar Series.* Upper Saddle river, N.J.: Prentice-Hall, Inc.

Chapter Two

Reading Activities

2.1 One Minute Story

Level: Intermediate-Advanced

Goal: Pre-reading, to interest students in the reading, speaking

Repetition Phrase: There is none for this activity, students just tell their one-minute stories.

Procedure:
1) Teacher gives students the main characters of the story they will be reading, and the setting or a few other details from the story without giving away the plot.
2) Students have one minute to guess what the story is about and draw it. They must write the main points of their story on the back of their drawing.
3) When students have finished their stories, they work in groups of four and re-tell their stories to their group members, referring to the main points they have written on the back of the drawing.
4) When all group members have told their stories, students in each group choose the story they think is closest to the real story to report to the class.
5) The student from each group whose story was chosen re-tells their story and shows his/her illustration to the class.
6) The class votes on the story that they believe is the closest to the real story.
7) Students read the story.
8) Students vote again on whose story was the closest to the real story.

Variation:
1) After step 8, students can make up various categories to give awards for the stories such as *funniest, most original, most unusual,* etc..
2) Students vote and teacher gives a ribbon or some kind of award to the winning students.

2.2 Re-Tell the Story

Level: Intermediate-Advanced

Goal: To reinforce reading comprehension by re-telling a reading

Repetition Phrase: There are no phrases, but students must say out loud what part of the story they are illustrating as they illustrate it.

NOTE: It is recommended to use a story with a lot of action or description

Procedure:
1) Teacher chooses a reading students have already read together or read as homework, and are familiar with. The reading should not be longer than 1-2 pages.
2) Teacher instructs students to draw what happened in the story, drawing key points that will help them remember the sequence of the story.
3) Teacher instructs students to say out loud what the parts of the story are as they draw it.
4) Teacher has students work in pairs. Student A must use his/her own drawing and re-tell the story in his/her own words to his/her partner.
5) After Student A has re-told the story, Student B may ask questions (in the target language only) about Student A's drawing and how it relates to the story.
6) Student B completes step 4 and Student A completes step 5.

Variation:
Teachers can have students summarize a chapter or a long reading by using several small pictures together, or by choosing their favorite part of the reading or most interesting, sad, funny, etc... part.

2.3 Main Idea

Level: Intermediate-Advanced

Goal: To summarize a reading, to identify the main idea of a reading, speaking

Repetition Phrase: The story is about _____.

Procedure:
1) Students are divided into groups of four and given different short readings in the target language.
2) Students read and then draw (or paint) a picture that summarizes the main idea of the reading.
3) While drawing or painting, students must repeat the repetition phrase inserting the main idea.

4) Students should write the main idea on the back of the illustration.
5) When all students have finished their illustrations of the main idea, students in each group take turns sharing their illustrations and main ideas, and discuss differences in opinion regarding the main idea of the story.
6) Students in each group are assigned a letter (A, B, C, D).
7) All students of the same letter must now move and sit together (all B's sit together, all C's, etc…). If there are more or less students of any letter, this is not a problem.
8) In each group, students take turns sharing their illustrations and versions of the main idea of the story.
9) After each student from each group has shared his/her main idea, students go back to their original groups.
10) One student in each original group must now report to his/her original group any main ideas that were different than what his/her group thought was the main idea and discuss which main idea seems to be the most accurate.
11) Students in each group vote on which main idea seems to be the most accurate.
12) One student from each group reports to the teacher the main idea his/her group chose, and the teacher writes the main idea on the board.
13) In plenary, students vote on which main idea is the most accurate (and grammatically correct).
14) Students in each group take turns re-reading the story out loud.

2.4 Main Characters

Level: Intermediate – Advanced

Goal: Reading comprehension, predicting, using descriptive language, speaking

Repetition Phrase: _____ is a _____, _____ woman/dog/ghost/man, etc. …

Procedure:
1) Choose a story with many different characters.
2) Have students read the story prior to class.

3) Students are assigned one character in the story (you will probably have several students with the same character – that is o.k.).
4) Students must choose several key adjectives to describe the character, and perhaps go back to the story to review the character's physical attributes and personality.
5) Students must illustrate their character repeating the character's name and several adjectives describing him/her (see repetition phrase) as they draw (or paint).
6) Students write their repetition phrase on the back.
7) Teacher circulates to ensure that the repetition phrases are correct.
8) Students find a partner.
9) Student A must look at Student B's drawing and try to guess the character and the adjectives used to describe that character.
10) When Student A has guessed correctly (or time is up), Student B shows the repetition phrase on the back and reads it to Student A. Student A repeats Student B's repetition phrase.
11) Students repeat step 8-10 with Student B looking at Student A's drawing.
12) When students have completed steps 8-10 twice, students find a new partner.
13) Students continue until time is up.

Variation:
1) After students have completed steps 1-13, in plenary, the teacher describes a character and students with that character must stand up and hold their illustration.
2) Teacher then collects all the character illustrations.
3) Teacher holds up a character and students must write the repetition phrase (or something similar that describes the character accurately).
4) Teacher collects the students' sentences and re-distributes them to other students.
5) Students work in groups of four and correct the sentences for grammar and accuracy.
6) Instead of painting or drawing, students can make a collage of their character. They can draw the character in the center, and glue items describing things about the character (example: what they like, what they like to do, their personality traits).
7) Instead of painting or drawing, students can make a mosaic of their character trying to incorporate their repetition phrase describing the character into the mosaic.

2.5 Art Jigsaw

Level: Intermediate – Advanced

Goal: Reading comprehension, speaking

Repetition Phrase: My section is about _____.

Procedure:
1) Divide a reading into four parts. Label each part A, B, C, D.
2) Teacher reviews difficult vocabulary with students.
3) Teacher distributes the four sections of the reading randomly.
4) Students must sit with students with the same reading (teacher directs all A's over here, all B's over there, etc...)
5) Students read the text, and discuss the meaning of the reading and write down the important facts.
6) Students draw a picture describing what happens in their section. While drawing, students repeat orally what their section is about (repetition phrase), practicing for their presentation to the new group.
7) Students must re-group so that every group has one A, one B, one C, one D (there is now someone that has read every section). If it works out that one or more groups don't have someone representing every section, the teacher must assign one student to cover two sections briefly.
8) Students in each group display their illustrations in the story sequence (what happened first goes first in the display). Each student shows their illustration and tells what their section of the story is about (see repetition phrase).
9) Each student must answer questions about their section.
10) In the same groups, students break into pairs. In each pair, the students take turns re-telling the entire reading. They may refer to the illustrations displayed and their repetition phrases if they can't remember the entire reading.
11) Students choose a favorite part of the reading and return to their original groups.
12) Students share their favorite part of the story.
13) Students re-read their original section and choose a favorite line.
14) Students share (and explain why they chose that line) their lines with the students from their original group.
15) In plenary, teacher and students discuss their favorite lines, and difficult sections of the reading.

2.6 Half and Half

Level: Intermediate – Advanced

Goal: Reading comprehension, making predictions, speaking

Repetition Phrase: "I think _____ happens in the beginning of the story."
OR "I think _____ will happen in the end of the story."

Procedure:
1) Teacher divides the class into two groups.
2) Teacher pre-teaches difficult vocabulary words.
3) One group is given the beginning of the story, and the other group is given the end of the story.
4) The group with the beginning of the story (Group A) must read the beginning, and discuss in groups what happened in the section they just read, and what they think will happen in the end.
5) Group A must illustrate what they think will happen in the end of the story. Students write their repetition phrase on the bottom of the illustration.
6) The group with the end of the story (Group B) must read the end and discuss in groups the section they read, and what they think will happen in the beginning of the story.
7) Group B must illustrate what they think will happen at the beginning of the story. Students write their repetition phrase on the bottom of the illustration.
8) Students must now find a partner from the opposite group and compare.
9) Students from Group A must show the student from Group B their ending and the student from Group B must show the student from Group A their beginning.
10) Students then share with each other the real ending or beginning.
11) Students find another partner and share their illustrations again, and take turns re-telling the section they read to their partner.
12) Students exchange readings and read the actual beginning or end (whatever they didn't read before).
13) Students find another partner and take turns re-telling the whole story in their own words.

2.7 Scrambled Reading

Level: Intermediate-Advanced

Goal: Reordering with coherence, reading comprehension

Repetition Phrase: (will vary) Students repeat aloud the main actions of the part of the story they are illustrating as they draw/paint it.

Procedure:
1) Choose a reading students are familiar with, that is easy to divide into parts.
2) Together, divide up the story into parts (according to the number of students). If the reading is short, you will need to divide the reading by sentences. If the reading is longer, you will need to divide it into sections. assign each student a part (you may want to let them choose the part they want).
3) Teachers instruct students to draw their section of the reading (dry media would be best since the drawings will be touched frequently in this activity).
4) While drawing, students need to repeat aloud the main points (or repeat the sentence they have been assigned) of their section.
5) If students are assigned only a sentence, they may write their sentence on the back of the illustration.
6) When time is up, the teacher collects all the drawings and mixes them up so they are not in the correct sequence of the story.
7) The teacher re-distributes the drawings being careful not to give a student his/her own drawing.
8) Students are instructed to look at the drawings and try to stand in front of the class in the proper sequence of the story.
9) Students who do not understand the meaning expressed in the drawings will need to find the illustrator of their drawing (using only the target language) and ask them questions about the drawing in order to clarify which section of the reading it is.
10) Students must work together to try to get the proper sequence. Teachers will need to circulate making sure that students are using the target language only.
11) When students are sure they have the correct order, they should line up in front of the class in the proper order

12) The first student then looks at his/her part of the story and tries to re-tell the section illustrated on their paper to the class. If the student makes mistakes, the original illustrator (the one who drew what was on their card) will need to step in and help them tell the section (or the line) of the story correctly.
13) When the first student has successfully re-told their section (or line) of the story the next student repeats step 12, and so on, until all students have re-told their line, or section of the story.
14) If at any time the story order is incorrect, the teacher must step in and help the students figure out which illustrations are in the wrong place.

Variation:

This works well with a very short story, or a very large class.

1) Divide students into small groups.
2) Each group must divide up work together and follow the procedure above (steps 3-10).
3) After students have completed step 10, they line up in their own own groups and re-tell the story.
4) After each group has re-told the story correctly among themselves, the teacher walks around and picks several people from each group (careful to pick only one person for each section) to come up and share their sections.
5) The students selected by the teacher quickly find their correct order in front of the classroom, and re-tell their section again in front of the class.

References:

Hess, N. & Pollard, L. (1997). *Zero Prep; Ready to Use Activities for the Language Classroom.* Burlingame, CA: Alta Books.

Chapter Three

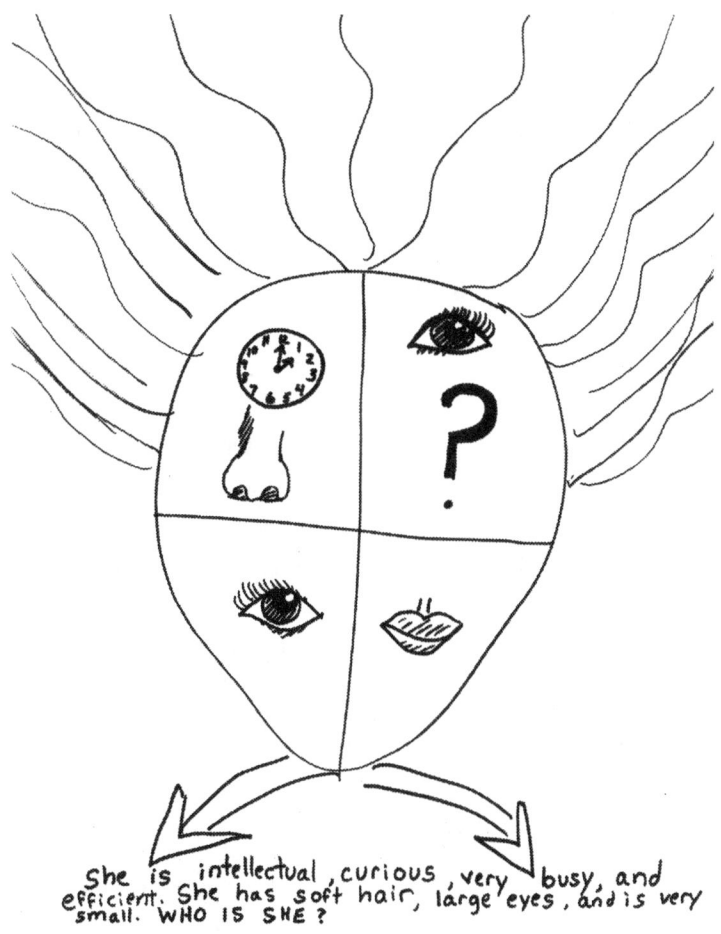

Writing Activities

3.1 Half and Half Writing

Level: Intermediate-Advanced

Goal: writing, speaking

Repetition Phrase: Say aloud what happens in the second part of the story.

Procedure:
1) Students are asked to close their eyes and try to form an image in their heads.
2) Teachers may want to assist in creating a mood by playing music or decorating the room with interesting decorations.
3) Students try to paint a picture of what they saw in their heads. If students could not come up with an idea in their heads, they could look around or walk around the building or campus, or the teacher could give some possible topics having to do with what they are studying in the textbook at that moment.
4) After students have completed their paintings, they must think of a story that goes with the painting.
5) Students write their story, but only the first half. While writing the story, students should be saying what they are drawing out loud.
6) Students are divided into two groups.
7) Group A receives Group B's first half, and Group B receives Group A's first half of the story.
8) Each group must now write the second half of the story from the student from the other group.
9) The teacher collects the first halves of the story, and puts them in a separate pile from the second halves.
10) Students help the teacher post the first halves on one side of the room, and the second halves on the other side.
11) Each group works as a team and must try to match the first half (by taking them off the wall and taping them together) with its counterpart. Students must first read all of the story parts in order to decide which ones go together.
12) The team who matches the most stories correctly first, wins.
13) After a winner has been declared, students re-attach the stories on the wall (the whole story this time) together with the painting of the first half, and students walk around the room reading the stories.

Variation:
1) Students could start by writing instead of painting. They would follow the steps just like above, but first write half of the story, then illustrate that half of the story.

2) Students would take their illustrations to a partner and the partner would try to guess the story. Then they would try to guess their partner's story.
3) Students then read their actual stories to their partners.
4) Students must then finish each other's story.
5) When students have finished their partner's story, they read the whole story to the partner, and then post the story (half from one student, half from the other) next to the painting for students to view.
6) When all students have finished posting their stories and paintings, students walk around the room reading each of the stories and looking at the paintings.

3.2 General Story Writing

Level: Intermediate – Advanced

Goal: writing, speaking

Repetition Phrase: Students repeat aloud the names of what they are drawing.

Procedure:
1) Teacher instructs students to form groups of four and brainstorm as many nouns as possible.
2) Students are instructed to choose five nouns and paint or draw them.
3) While students are painting or drawing, they must repeat aloud the names of the nouns they are drawing.
4) Students are divided into pairs (with students from different groups).
5) In pairs, students trade drawings with each other.
6) Students must now look at their partner's drawing (or painting) and write a story incorporating those nouns.
7) When students have finished their stories, they take turns reading their stories to their partner.
8) Students place the illustrations next to the stories written about them and display them around the room for students to read.
9) Students walk around the room reading the stories.

Variation:
1) Students complete steps 1-3.

2) Students choose one painting or drawing from each group. That drawing is displayed somewhere on the group's desks.
3) Each student in each group is given a letter, A, B, C, D.
4) All students go and form a new group with students that have the same letter (all A students sit together, all B students, etc…). Students leave the chosen painting or drawing from each group where it was.
5) Students in the new groups must look at the drawing or painting that is displayed in their group's area and write a story about the drawing or painting.
6) When students are finished, students in each group take turns reading their stories to their group members.

3.3 Art Missing Words Dictacomp

Level: Intermediate – Advanced

Goal: listening, writing, vocabulary

Repetition Phrase: _____ is _____. (The definition of the word they are illustrating).

Procedure:
1) Teacher chooses a short reading that students are familiar with.
2) Teacher writes difficult vocabulary on the board, and discusses the words with students.
3) Teacher assigns each student one vocabulary word to illustrate.
4) Students illustrate their word and repeat the definition of the word or use the word in a sentence (repetition phrase) while they draw.
5) Teacher collects the drawings.
6) Teacher reads the selected reading to students aloud 3 times.
7) Teacher starts out reading slowly and increases speed with each reading (students should be listening the first time, and taking notes the second or third time).
8) Teacher reads the reading a fourth time leaving out the key vocabulary words. Instead of the vocabulary word, the teacher holds up the drawing of the word that one of the students made.

9) Students must try to guess the vocabulary word that was left out by memory, or by looking at the student's drawing.
10) After the teacher has finished reading, students work in groups of four and compare to see if they have guessed the missing words correctly.
11) Teacher reads the story one last time holding up the drawings again.
12) Students work together and try to re-create the entire reading. Each group should have only one re-created reading.
13) Students compare their work with the other groups.
14) Students post their re-created readings around the room and students walk around and read them.
15) Students vote on which story came closest to the original. Students may refer to the original reading (from their textbooks or handout) to decide which reading is closest.
16) Teacher circulates and helps students understand mistakes they made in re-creating the story.

3.4 Student Art Dictacomp

Level: Beginning-Advanced

Goal: writing, speaking, vocabulary, review of verbs in the simple past, present progressive, prepositions and other location words.

Repetition Phrase: Students say aloud what they are drawing in their picture.

Procedure:
1) Teacher gives students a theme based on the unit students are studying (example: transportation or food).
2) Students must draw a picture including as many vocabulary words as possible that they have learned regarding the topic.
3) While students are drawing (or painting), they must repeat aloud the words they are including in their drawing.
4) Teacher gives students 10 minutes to write complete sentences describing what is in the picture they drew (or painted). Students may use prepositions of location, action verbs, anything they want to describe the picture.
5) Students are grouped into pairs.

6) Students exchange drawings (or paintings) and are given 5 minutes to study each other's drawings.
7) After time is called, students return the drawing to the other student, and return to their seats.
8) Students must now write complete sentences describing what was in the <u>other</u> student's picture. Students may use prepositions of location, action verbs, anything they want to describe what was in the picture.
9) Students return to their partner and take turns comparing what they both wrote about each drawing (or painting).
10) Students work together and try to correct the grammar in each other's sentences. Teacher circulates to facilitate grammar correction.

3.5 What's Different

Level: Beginning-Intermediate

Goal: writing, speaking

Repetition Phrase: Students say aloud the names of the nouns included in the pictures.

Procedure:
1) Students are divided into pairs.
2) Each pair of students must choose a scene to draw based on something they are studying in the textbook. The scene should include recently learned vocabulary words.
3) Teacher must remind students to keep the drawings simple, but include at least 15 nouns in the picture.
4) While students are drawing they must repeat the names of the nouns in the picture (repetition phrase).
5) The pair of students must work together to make their drawings the same, except make 5 differences. For example, they could both draw a flower but on one student's drawing the flower is pink, and on the other student's drawing the flower is yellow. The students must write the 5 differences (in complete sentences) on a separate piece of paper.
6) When students have completed their drawings, they merge with another pair of students.

7) Each pair must exchange drawings with the other pair, and return to their seats.
8) The pairs are given 5 minutes to come up with the five differences between the drawings and write them down in complete sentences.
9) When the five minutes are up, students go back to the other pair whose drawing they have and read the sentences they wrote about the differences.
10) Students compare to see if they guessed the differences correctly, and ask questions about the drawings.

Variation:
1) Students can bring magazines or any kind of pictures to class and work individually.
2) Students choose a picture from the magazine and try to copy the picture changing 5 things. Students write the 5 changes in complete sentences on a separate piece of paper.
3) Students work in pairs and try to guess the other student's 5 changes by looking at their magazine picture and their copied picture together.
4) Students write the changes they have found in complete sentences.
5) Students meet back with their partner and read their sentences.
6) Students check each other's work and ask questions.

3.6 Wanted Criminals

Level: Beginning-intermediate

Goal: writing, to review present perfect, descriptive adjectives

Repetition Phrase: Students say aloud the sentences they write to describe their criminal.

Procedure:
1) Students are divided into groups of four.
2) Students are told that there is a terrible criminal on the loose, and students must make WANTED posters to distribute.
3) Students work together in groups to describe their criminal.

4) Students must write 10 sentences about the criminal (together). Students are encouraged to use descriptive adjectives to physically describe the criminal, and give vital information like height, weight, etc.
5) Students must also give a brief history of what the criminal has done to be put on the WANTED list. Teacher must point out the use of the present perfect for this part, by giving students an example. A possible example might be: She has robbed 10 gas stations so far. People have seen her in Omaha, Council Bluffs, and Norfolk. She has escaped from prison 2 times.
6) Each student must now make a WANTED poster for their criminal. Students first copy the sentences they wrote in groups onto the bottom of the poster.
7) Students then draw their criminal. While students draw they need to repeat out loud the description of the criminal.
8) Students choose a representative from the group to read the criminal's description to the class.
9) After each group has read their description, students display their posters around the room. Students from each group should display their posters next to each other.
10) Students walk around the room comparing the posters from each group and reading the descriptions.

3.7 Abstractions

Level: Beginning- Intermediate

Goal: writing, review of descriptive adjectives, giving compliments

Repetition Phrase: This person is _____, _____, and _____.

Procedure:
1) Students write their names on a small strip of paper and give them to the teacher.
2) Teacher re-distributes the names so that all students have the name of a different student.

3) Teacher tells students they must paint an abstract portrait of the person whose name is on their paper.

4) It might be helpful for the teacher to provide an example on the computer, or show an actual print. Teachers can use www.abcgallery.com to look up Picasso's "Girl Before a Mirror" or Matisse's "The Green Line – *La Raie verte*" or any other abstract portraits of the teacher's choice. As students draw, they must say aloud or to themselves, sentences describing the person in the painting. These sentences should be compliments. They can be funny, but nothing negative.

5) Students then take their painting back to their own desk and on a separate piece of paper write 5-7 sentences that are clues describing their partner. These sentences must accurately describe the person so that students can guess who it is, but should not completely give away the student's identity. Students must repeat these sentences out loud or to themselves as they are writing them. Students should write the person's name on the back of the paper with the sentences. Teacher should circulate to correct mistakes in the sentences.

6) Teacher calls on students one at a time to stand up and hold up their painting.

7) The student holding up the painting must read the sentences describing the person in the painting, and students must try to guess who it is.

8) The student holding up the painting must tell the class when they guess correctly, and give the painting and the sentences to the person who was painted (to take home as a souvenir).

9) Continue until students have guessed who the people in all the paintings are.

Variation:
1) Have students write sentences about the people using vocabulary that is currently being learned in class.
2) Have students write sentences about the people using certain verb tenses currently being studied in class.

3.8 Three Part Story

Level: Intermediate-Advanced

Goal: writing

Repetition Phrase: (will vary) Students repeat aloud whatever they are drawing or painting.

Procedure:
   * Wet media is suggested for this activity.
   1) Teacher instructs students to put their head on the desk and close their eyes.
   2) Teacher plays music in the target language, or plays the sound from a video in the target language.
   3) Teacher instructs students to listen to the sounds and form a picture of a person, place, or thing, in their head.
   4) When the teacher turns off the music or whatever sounds were being played, students are instructed to paint the image they formed in their heads.
   5) When time is up, students are divided into groups of three.
   6) In each group, the students hang up, or display (for their group) their own paintings so the three paintings are placed side by side.
   7) Students are instructed to use the three paintings to write a short story. They must incorporate each of the paintings somehow into their story.
   8) When students are finished writing their stories, they must display them next to the three paintings they used as a muse.
   9) Students go around the room reading each other's stories and looking at the the art they used to create them.

Variation:
   1) Follow steps 1-7.
   2) Teacher takes the three paintings from each groups and puts them on display in the back of the room. Teacher gives a number to each groups' artwork and labels each groups' artwork with the number.
   3) Students display their stories separately from the paintings.
   4) Students must read each other's stories and try to guess which group's artwork they used to create the story. They record their guess by writing the number of the group's artwork on the students' story.

5) In plenary, the teacher hands back each story to the author, and as a class, they check to see if students guessed the correct artwork.
6) Students explain (in the target language) how they used the artwork to write their story.

References:

Hess, N. & Pollard, L. (1997). *Zero Prep; Ready to Use Activities for the Language Classroom.* Burlingame, CA: Alta Books.

Matisse, Henri.(1905). *Madame Matisse "The Green Line"* (*La Raie verte*). Oil on canvas, Statens Museum for Kunst, Copenhagen, Denmark.

Picasso, Pablo. (1932). *Girl Before a Mirror.* Oil on canvas. The Museum of Modern Arts, New York, NY, USA.

Woodward, S. (1997). *Fun With Grammar; Communicative Activities for the Azar Grammar Series.* Upper Saddle river, N.J.: Prentice-hall,Inc.

Chapter Four

Grammar Activities

4.1 Simple Present

Level: Beginning

Goal: To practice the simple present with action verbs (practice conjugations with certain languages). To review expressions of habitual actions like at night, in the morning, in the evening, once a week, twice a month, etc..

Repetition Phrase: I _____ at night.
John _____ in the morning.

Special Materials: Small paper bag or box

Procedure:
1) Students review with teacher action verbs and expressions of habitual actions (and simple present conjugations if applicable).
2) Teacher assigns each student a verb and a subject. Students must conjugate the verb correctly in a sentence and write it on the bottom of their drawing paper.
3) Students illustrate their sentence (painting or drawing) and repeat the repetition phrase while drawing.
4) Students are divided into groups of four students each.
5) In each group, students take turns holding up their illustration (but covering the repetition phrase) for students to guess the repetition phrase.
6) Students guess the repetition phrase and the student holding up the illustration reveals if they are correct.
7) All students in the group repeat the correct repetition phrase of the student holding up the illustration.
8) When all students have had a chance for the group to guess their repetition phrase, students in each group put their illustrations together in a pile facing down.
9) One student from the group draws a picture and acts it out.
10) The other students in the group try to guess the repetition phrase that the student is trying to act out (Example: I eat pizza on Friday nights.).
11) When all students have had a turn, students go back to their seats.
12) Students cut off their repetition phrases from the bottom of the illustration.
13) Students display their illustrations around the room, and put their repetition phrases in the teacher's paper bag or box.
14) Teacher walks around the room and students draw one repetition phrase from the box or bag, teacher is careful not to give a student his/her own repetition phrase.

Chapter 4: Grammar Activities   51

15) Students are given two minutes to find the illustration that matches the repetition phrase.
16) Students stand by the illustration that matches their repetition phrase.
17) Students go around the room saying their repetition phrase while students look at the illustration they are standing by.

Variation:

Students can do the same activity, but instead of drawing, they can make diagrams using old tissue boxes. Teachers would have to ask students to bring their own boxes and anything they would like to use to make their diagram. Students then use the diagrams for this activity instead of the pictures. Students will need to write their repetition phrases on a small piece of paper.

4.2 Be/Have

Level: Beginning- Intermediate)

Goal: To review the verbs be, and have (for beginners, review only in present tense, for intermediate, review future as well) and to review descriptive adjectives

Repetition Phrases: Example: The girl has three buttons on her shirt. OR The man has a mustache. OR The woman is very old.

Procedure:
1) The day before the activity, the teacher tells students to choose a person they admire to illustrate. It can be anyone from real life, T.V. or movies.
2) Students paint a picture of this person careful to add at least 10 recognizable details to the painting.
3) Students should not worry if their painting is good, just worry about putting in details that students can recognize.
4) While painting, students should be saying out loud the repetition phrases regarding the details used in the painting. These sentences should include the verbs "have" or "be".
5) Students write their repetition phrases on the back of the painting (wait until the painting is dry to write them).
6) Students bring their artwork to class the next day.
7) In pairs, students look at each other's artwork.

8) Student A tries to say as many sentences using the verbs "be" and "have" that describe the painting.
9) Teacher circulates to make sure students are forming the sentences correctly.
10) When Student A can't think of any more sentences, Student B reveals his/her repetition phrases and both students repeat them together.
11) Student B completes step 7 - 10.
12) Students find another partner and continue steps 7-11.
13) Students continue from partner to partner until time is up.

4.3 Present Progressive – Picture Descriptions

Level: Beginning

Goal: To review the present progressive, action verbs, vocabulary

Repetition Phrase: The boy is _____. The ducks are _____. (Students create sentences in the present progressive based on the drawings).

Special Materials: Colored markers or pens

Procedure:
1) The teacher tells students the theme of the unit they are working on in the textbook. (Example: transportation, cities, food, clothing)
2) Students draw a scene incorporating as many words from that unit as possible. In the scene, people must be performing different actions (tell students to try to use the action verbs they have learned).
3) While students are drawing they should be creating sentences in the present progressive. Students should repeat those sentences aloud, and when the drawing is completed, they should copy those sentences on a separate piece of paper.
4) Students are divided into groups of 4.
5) Students take turns holding up their pictures while their group members shout out sentences in the present progressive describing what is happening in the picture.
6) When all students in the group have held up their pictures, students display their drawings where their group can see them.

7) Each student is given a different colored pen and a captain of each group is chosen.
8) Students start with the first drawing displayed and take one paper and pass it from student to student within their group.
9) Each student must write (in their colored marker or pen) one sentence in the present progressive about the designated drawing.
10) When all students have written about the designated drawing, the captain picks up the paper and puts it with the designated drawing. The captain then chooses another drawing, and students repeat steps 8-9 until all the drawings have been written about.
11) Captains choose one of the group's drawings and sentences to share with the class.
12) Captains take turn sharing the drawings with the sentences in the present progressive.

4.4 Present Progressive – Imagine

Level: Beginning

Goal: To review the present progressive

Repetition Phrases:
"I am in Jamaica. I am snorkeling."
"Mom is in Egypt. She is visiting the pyramids."
(Sentences will vary depending on the drawing and the person.)

Procedure:
1) Students are given a subject (I, you, he/she, it, we, they, you plural). Teachers can walk around and assign each student a subject, or the students can write a subject on a slip of paper and turn it into the teacher. The teacher would then re-distribute these slips of paper so everyone has a subject, but not the one they wrote.
2) If students are given "I", they must think of a place they would like to go.
3) If students are given "you", they must think of a place they think the teacher would like to go.
4) If they are given "he/she" they must choose a person they know well, and think of a place he/she would like to go.

5) If they are given "it" they must think of a pet or animal they know well.
6) If they are given "we" they must think of a few good friends and think of a place all of them (the student included) would like to go.
7) If they are given "they", they must think of a few good friends and think of a place all of them would like to go.
8) When the student has a place in mind, the student must think of something his/her subject(s) would be doing in that place.
9) The student must now draw the person(s) at the place they would like to be, doing what they would like to do.
10) The student must repeat the repetition phrases while drawing (these phrases will be different, but should include the location, the subjects, and what they are doing). Students should copy the repetition phrases on the back of the drawing.
11) Students walk around and find a partner.
12) Students ask the partner who the subject is, where they are, and what they are doing. Teacher should model these questions on the board first, so students know exactly what to ask, and can refer to them later if needed.
13) After they have each asked the questions and answered them, students get new partners.
14) Continue until teacher calls time.
15) Teacher collects pictures with the repetition phrases on the back.
16) Teacher holds up drawings and calls on students to tell her/him what the people are doing in the picture.
17) Teacher holds up drawings and asks students questions about the drawings (Example: Where are they? What are they doing? Who is it?)

4.5 Simple Past

Level: Intermediate

Goal: To review the simple past in context, especially irregular verbs

Repetition Phrase: Use the verb in a sentence in the past tense according to the subject assigned.

Procedure:
1) Students review the formation of the simple past, and irregular verbs.

2) Each student is assigned an irregular verb and a subject.
3) The students must draw a picture illustrating the subject and the verb. While drawing, students need to write on the front and say their verb (conjugated to the assigned subject) in the present tense, and then turn their paper over and use the verb in a sentence in the simple past. Students must repeat this sentence aloud (repetition phrase).
4) Students mingle around the room looking for partners.
5) Student A looks at Student B's picture and repeats the verb in the present tense.
6) Student A then says the verb in the simple past, and formulates his/her own sentence using the verb in the past tense.
7) Student B shares his/her sentence with Student A.
8) Student B now must look at Student A's drawing and repeat steps 5-7.
9) Students find new partners and continue until time is up.
10) The teacher collects all the drawings and holds them up one at a time for students to see. Students read aloud the verbs in the present, and shout out the simple past.
11) If time, the teacher holds up some drawings and calls on individual students to use the verb in the simple past in a sentence.

Variation:
1) Students complete steps 1-3.
2) Students stand in two lines facing each other.
3) Students complete steps 5-8.
4) Teacher plays music and students in one line (designated by the teacher) move down one person to the left (the person on the left end must go to the right end of the line so that everyone has a new partner). Students must dance to the music as they move. Teacher should play upbeat music in the target language.

4.6. Simple Past - An Embarrassing Thing That Happened

Level: Intermediate – Advanced

Goal: To review the simple past in context, to tell a story, speaking, writing

Repetition Phrase: I _____. (Tell main idea of embarrassing story)

Procedure:
- This activity works well when following activity 4.5.

1) Students are told to put their heads down on the desk.
2) They are to take 3 minutes to think of an embarrassing thing that happened to them.
3) When time is up, students must paint the main idea of what happened to them (Example: I fell down in front of 50 people. OR My pants were unzipped on the stage.)
4) Students must write the main idea on the bottom of the painting, and repeat this sentence as they are painting.
5) When students have completed their paintings, they are divided into groups of 4 students.
6) In each group, students take turns looking at each other's pictures, and listening to the stories.
7) Now each group member is given a letter (A, B, C, D) and told to sit with students who have the same letter as them (all A's together, all B's together, etc...).
8) Students in their new groups repeat step 6.
9) Students in each group vote on the MOST embarrassing story.
10) In plenary, students whose stories were voted as the MOST embarrassing get in front of the class and tell their stories to the whole class.
11) Students are assigned to write their stories as homework.

Variation:
1) Instead of voting on the most embarrassing story, students return to their seats and the teacher asks for volunteers to share their stories.
2) Volunteers get up one at a time and share their stories to the class.

4.7 Past Progressive

Level: Intermediate – Advanced

Goal: To review the past progressive, speaking

Repetition Phrase: Students think of a sentence for the poster using the past progressive (Example: At 8 o'clock last night, I was studying.).

Special Materials: 4-5 pieces of poster paper (enough for each group) and markers

Procedure:
1) Teacher reviews with students the current chapter's theme, and the formation of the past progressive. Students are divided into groups of 3-4 people.
2) Each group decides on an idea for the poster.
3) The idea must be a picture of many people doing many activities.
4) Students divide up the items in the picture so that they are all drawing something different. As they draw, students should be thinking of a sentence in the past progressive that goes with what they are drawing. Students should repeat these sentences aloud (but quietly so as not to disturb the people in their group).
5) Teacher should be circulating to make sure that students are repeating their repetition phrases aloud, and using the past progressive correctly.
6) When students have completed their posters, the teacher collects them and re-distributes them to another group.
7) Now each group has a new picture.
8) Each group has 5 minutes to write (on a separate piece of paper) as many sentences as possible about the picture in the past progressive.
9) When time is up, students share their sentences with the class and get points for each correct sentence that correctly describes the picture. Students then pass their poster to the next group and receive a new poster from another group.
10) Students repeat steps 8-9 until all groups have had a chance to write about all the groups' posters.
11) Students add up the points and the group with the most points wins.

Variation:
1) Teacher collects all the posters and holds up one at a time.
2) Students complete steps 8-9 using the same picture. Students continue until all posters have been written about.

4.8 Verb Tense Review - Remember the Song

Level: Intermediate – Advanced

Goal: To review any tense students are currently working on, depending on the song chosen.

Repetition Phrase: This song is about _____.

Special Materials: A song and stereo or computer to play the song, and copies of the song's lyrics (these can be found easily on the internet).

Procedure:
1) Teacher tells students they are going to listen to a song in the target language. Students need to listen only the first time.
2) The second time the teacher plays the music, students need to write down any words or phrases they can pick out from the song.
3) The third time, students listen to the song, students draw what they think the song is about, or anything the song inspires them to draw.
4) Students finish their drawings after the teacher stops playing the song.
5) Students write what they think the song is about (repetition phrase) on the bottom of the drawing, and say aloud the repetition phrase as they are drawing.
6) When students have completed their drawings, they form groups of 3 or 4 students and discuss any words they picked up from the song, and discuss what they think the song is about.
7) Students are given letters A,B,C,D and are told to sit with students of the same letter (all A's sit together, all B's sit together, etc…).
8) In the new groups, students share their drawings and repetition phrases and explain why they came to that conclusion (the meaning of the song).
9) Students are encouraged to form sentences in the discussion using the tense they are reviewing (Examples: past progressive – He was sitting on the bed when the phone rang. Future – The song is about what he will do if his wife leaves him).
10) In each group, students vote on which summary of the song is the most accurate.
11) In plenary, representatives from each group report to the class about the summary that was chosen from their group.

Chapter 4: Grammar Activities   59

12) Teacher passes out the lyrics to the song, and students and teacher discuss the meaning together, and which tense the verbs are in. Students then vote on which student's summary was the closest.
13) Students sing the song together.

4.9 Present Perfect

Level: Intermediate-Advanced

Goal: To practice and improve understanding of the use of the present perfect.

Repetition Phrase: I've never _____. (gone to a movie, jumped off the Empire State Building, etc...)

Procedure:
1) Teacher instructs students to draw a picture of something they have never done before. It could be something they don't want to do, or something they would like to do in the future.
2) Students must say "I've never _____" while they are drawing.
3) Students sit in a circle with their pictures.
4) A scorekeeper is chosen to write each student's name on the board and then record his/her points under it.
5) The first student holds up his/her picture and says the repetition phrase. (Example: I've never been to Africa.)
6) Going around the circle, each student must repeat this repetition phrase if it is true. If it isn't true (that is, they HAVE been to Africa) they must say "pass" and the student whose repetition phrase it is gets a point for each student that says "pass".
7) If at any point any student is believed to be lying, another student may say "I challenge you." The student must then provide evidence supporting their statement (such as, "I went to Asia, not Africa. I am from Turkey, not Africa.) If the student cannot be proven to be lying, the game continues. If the student can be proven to be lying, then the challenger gets the point.
8) After the first student has let every student repeat his/her repetition phrase, it is the next student in the circle's turn.

9) This continues until all students have had a chance to do every student's repetition phrase and see the drawings with it.
10) The scorekeeper calculates the points and the student with the most points wins.

Note: Students are encouraged to avoid personal issues.

4.10 Future- Future Progressive

Level: Intermediate

Goal: To review the future and future progressive and use it in context, speaking

Repetition Phrases: Ten years from now, I will be _____.(in Las Vegas, married with 3 children, traveling around the world, etc…)

Procedure:
1) Students are given 5 minutes to review the future and future progressive in groups of 4 or 5.
2) Students are told to think of what they would like to be doing and where they would like to be (or where they think they will be and what they think they will be doing) 10 years from now.
3) Students must paint or draw where they will be in 10 years, and what they will be doing.
4) While students are drawing or painting, they need to repeat the repetition phrases. Students need to make sure their repetition phrases include the simple future (to say where they will be), the future progressive (to say what they are doing). Students may also choose to include a sentence in the simple future using –be with an adjective (Example: I will be in New York. I will be studying music. I will be single.)
5) Students must copy their repetition phrases on a separate piece of paper. The teacher must circulate to make sure students are repeating the repetition phrases, and with languages that have future endings, make sure students are putting the correct endings onto the verbs.
6) The teacher walks around the room and writes a number on the back of each painting and on the front of each paper of repetition phrases. Each student's painting and repetition phrases should have the same number.

7) Students display the paintings and the repetition phrases separately around the room.
8) Students are divided into pairs. The pairs walk around the room looking at the paintings and the repetition phrases.
9) In pairs, students try to find the painting that matches the repetition phrases.
10) When time is up, the teacher walks around pointing to a painting, and students must shout out the number of the repetition phrases page that they think the painting matches.
11) A student volunteer follows the teacher and when students have called out the correct paper that matches the painting, the student takes the paper and attaches it next to the painting.
12) This continues until all paintings have been matched up with the correct papers.
13) The teacher divides the class into two groups.
14) Group A stands by their paintings and phrases.
15) Group B goes and stands by a person from Group A, so that everyone has a partner.
16) Students from Group B ask students from Group A questions about their painting or about their life in the future using the future or future progressive.
17) Students from Group A answer the questions and then read their repetition phrase to their partner.
18) Teacher rings a bell or whistles, and all students move down one (so everyone has a new partner) and students repeat steps 16-18.
19) Continue until all Group B students have seen all of Group A's paintings.
20) Teacher calls on Group B to stand by their paintings, and students repeat steps 16-19.

4.11 Future – What Happens Next?

Level: Intermediate

Goal: To review the simple future, speaking

Repetition Phrase: What will happen next? I think _____ will _____.
   (will vary depending on the drawing)

Special Materials: Have students bring magazines of people.

Procedure:
1) Teacher reviews with students the formation of the simple future.
2) Students are divided into four groups.
3) In each group, students put all their magazines in the center of the table or on one student's desk, for use by all students in the group.
4) Students are directed to find one interesting picture of a character completing some kind of action that might cause something else to happen (Example: A man is walking on the street and a woman in an apartment above is beginning to water her plants). Teachers will want to model this by putting several pictures on the board, and then asking students what they think will happen next. Teachers will want to explain that they will be looking for the same kind of picture, and the other students will be guessing what will happen next.
5) When all students have glued their pictures onto a piece of paper, teacher collects them.
6) Teacher re-distributes all the papers so that each student now has a different picture.
7) Students must imagine what they think might happen next in the picture, and draw it on the back of the paper.
8) Students must write what they think will happen next (using the simple future) under their illustration.
9) In plenary, the teacher collects all the pictures and calls a student to come to the front and hold up his/her picture.
10) Students shout out what they think will happen next in the picture.
11) The student then turns the picture over and shows the illustration and reads the sentence he/she wrote underneath it.
12) Continue until time is up, or until all students have shared their illustrations.

Variation:
1) Complete step 1 from above.
2) Teacher puts a picture on the computer, or holds one up, and ask students "What will happen next?
3) Students draw a picture of what they think will happen next.
4) While drawing, students repeat the repetition phrase and write it on the back.

5) Students mingle asking each other "What do you think will happen next?" and students read their repetition phrases to each other and show their pictures.
6) Complete steps 9-12 from above.

4.12 Review of Tenses

Level: Advanced

Goal: To review all tenses, speaking

Repetition Phrases: These phrases will vary in tense from group to group, and vary in subject from person to person. See procedures for examples.

Procedure:
1) Teacher tells students they will be reviewing tenses today.
2) Teacher divides the room into 6 groups. Teacher designates one tense to every group and has a student write the name of the tense and an example on a piece of paper in the middle of the group's desks. The tenses to be reviewed can be the following; simple present, present perfect, past perfect, past progressive, future, future perfect. The teacher may want to choose other tenses instead.
3) Teacher tells students to sit in the group that has the tense they need to work on most.
4) In that group, students work together to create sentences about themselves using that tense.
5) When students have written the sentences on a piece of paper, they choose one (making sure that each student chooses a different one) and illustrate it.
6) Students repeat the sentence aloud as they illustrate.
7) Students walk around the room and read their sentences and show their pictures to each other. Students need to make sure the other student understands the meaning of their sentence.
8) Students continue with step 7 until all students have seen at least 10 sentences.
9) In plenary, teacher calls on students to hold up their drawings.
10) Teacher asks the student holding up the drawing what tense their sentence is in.

11) Students try to guess the sentence, or try to form any sentence about the picture in that tense.
12) Continue until time is up.

4.13 Questions

Level: Beginning – Advanced

Goal: To practice forming questions, speaking, writing

Repetition Phrase: Students will repeat aloud what is happening in the picture while they are drawing it.

Procedure:
1) Teacher assigns students to draw or paint something based on a theme from their current unit in the textbook. Students are told to include a lot of activity.
2) While students are drawing, they must repeat aloud what is happening in the drawing/ painting.
3) Students bring their painting/drawing to class the next day.
4) Teacher divides students into pairs.
5) Teacher reviews question words that he/she wants to target (such as how, why, how much, when, where, etc…) and specifies a tense (for beginning students present/present progressive, for intermediate students, past, past progressive, and for advanced students, conditional, subjunctive, future progressive, etc…).
6) Student A looks at Student B's picture and asks five questions about it using the teacher's specifications.
7) Student B answers the questions.
8) Student B asks Student A five questions about Student A's picture.
9) Student A answers the questions.
10) Students find another partner and repeat steps 6-9.
11) Students are now divided into groups of 4.
12) In each group, one students holds up their picture, and the other students may each ask one question about it. The person holding up the picture must answer the questions.

13) Continue until all students in each group have held up a picture and answered the questions.
14) In each group, one drawing is chosen, and all the students work together to write five questions about that drawing (only one paper is needed per group).
15) In plenary, teacher asks students from each group to write their five written questions on the board.
16) Teacher gives the class a chance to correct other students' work by giving the entire class five minutes. In those five minutes, students must go up to the board and make any changes they think are necessary to the questions.
17) Teacher has students read their questions aloud, making corrections if the class was unable to correct the errors themselves.
18) Teacher calls on the students whose pictures the questions were about, to answer the questions (in plenary).

Variation:
1) For more advanced students, teacher doesn't specify question words or tenses, students just choose what comes natural when looking at the picture.

4.14 Questions-Commercials

Level: Intermediate- Advanced

Goal: To practice forming, asking and answering questions

Repetition Phrase: Students will repeat aloud the questions they have formed for their commercial.

Special Materials: Students will need time outside of class to work on the commercials, and any materials needed for their commercial, also, if students and teacher choose to film the commercials, students will need a video camera.

Procedure:
1) Teacher announces that students need to think of an invention that they would like to have.
2) Students do not need to create the actual models of the inventions, they just need to think of an invention that would be useful to them.

3) Students need to create a commercial to sell their inventions.
4) Teacher needs to model an example commercial for an invention on the board.
5) Students are told to follow the example when writing their commercials. That is, each commercial should be no longer than 3 minutes, and include three introductory questions for the audience.

>   Example:
>   1) Do you ever wake up so happy and peaceful because you had a wonderful dream?
>   2) Do you have dreams you wish you could repeat?
>   3) Have you ever wanted to stay in your dream forever?
>
>   Well! Now's your chance! With one click on the HP handheld dream retriever, your dreams can be re-created again, and again! Call now at 1-800-DREAM to order!

6) Students are told that their commercials can be performed live or on video, and teacher must give students a few days to prepare their presentations.
7) Teacher gives students a few moments in class to formulate possible questions for their commercials, and teacher circulates to correct grammar.
8) Students are instructed that as they prepare the visual part of their commercial (artwork or pictures, or downloaded pictures or action shots) they must practice their questions aloud. Also, students must provide the class with a copy of the transcripts of the presentation.
9) On the day the commercials are due, students present their commercials and distribute the transcripts to the other students.
10) After each presentation, the teacher and students look over the transcripts and check for grammar mistakes, especially in the formulation of the questions.

Variation:
1) Students complete all steps as written above, but work in groups of 3-4 students to create one commercial for each group.
2) Students may film the commercials and present them in class at a later date, or take several class periods to create the commercials, and present them live in class.

4.15 Count/Non- Count

Level: Beginning – Intermediate

Goal: To review the use of count/non-count nouns and expressions of quantity

Repetition PhraseS: Students repeat the word they are illustrating to themselves and say whether it is count or non-count. When students are writing sentences in teams, they must look at the illustration for the word they are making a sentence for and say the sentence aloud.

Procedure:
1) Teacher reviews the meaning of count/non-count nouns, and yells out words from the following list as students yell out COUNT or NON-COUNT:

    (Non-Count)
    furniture, money, mail, jewelry, sugar, coffee, bread, sunshine, luck, water, tea, milk, steam, air, smoke, pollution, rice, chalk, corn, dirt, dust, grass

    (Count)
    apple, car, book, boy, girl, tables, mountain, lake, telephone, kitchen, baby, vegetable, office, morning, street, newspaper, bedroom, hotel, bicycle, chicken, airplane

2) Teacher assigns each student a word from the list or from the student's text to illustrate. He/she does not tell the student if the word is count or non-count. At the bottom of the illustration, students must write the name of the word.
3) After students have illustrated their word, they are divided into groups of four.
4) Teacher tells students they must sort all the words in their group according to count or non-count. The first team that finishes with the words in the correct list wins.
5) After students have sorted their words and the teacher has found the winners and checked all students lists for accuracy, teacher writes this list of modifiers on the board; some, a, an, two, a lot of, many, much.
6) Students must work together in their groups and come up with a sentence for each of the count/non-count words using one of the modifiers (Example: I have a lot of milk in my fridge.)

7) When teacher calls time, the teams put their team name on the board and write their sentences underneath.
8) Teacher gives students five minutes to look over their team's sentences for errors and correct them. Students are encouraged to work together.
9) In plenary, students take turns reading their sentences to the class. The class decides if the sentences are correct or not (unless they get it wrong, then the teacher steps in). If the sentence is correct, the team gets a point. If it is not correct, the class and teacher discuss why, and correct the sentence, but they do not get a point.
10) After all the sentences have been corrected, teacher writes on the board again this list of modifiers; some, a, an, two, a lot of, many, much.
11) Teacher writes up this chart and calls on students to fill in the chart for a particular modifier (Example: Juan, where would some go on this chart? - Answer: under plural count nouns, and non-count nouns)

	Singular	plural
Count noun		
Non-count noun		_____

12) Students should have figured out how they can use the modifiers from the activity. If students make mistakes, teachers should ask students to refer to the sentences on the board for help. Teacher then summarizes the use of the modifiers with count and non-count nouns.

4.16 Prepositions

Level: Beginning-Intermediate

Goal: To review prepositions of location

Repetition Phrases:
   The flowers are in the garden.
   The car is in front of the house.
   The cat is under the chair.
   (These will vary depending on each student's drawing)

Procedure:
1) Teacher has students write as many prepositions of location that they can think of on the right side of the chalkboard.
2) On the left side of the chalkboard, each student must write one noun that might be found in or around a house (such as flowers, door, car, cat).
3) Students are told to draw or paint a picture of a house. They must then choose ten nouns and put the nouns somewhere in the picture.
4) While students are drawing or painting, they must describe aloud the location of the nouns using the prepositions listed on the board (these are the repetition phrases).
5) When students have completed their pictures, they must find a partner or teacher assigns partners.
6) Student A looks at Student B's picture and tries to describe the location of each of the nouns in the picture (using the correct prepositions).
7) Student B refers to the repetition phrases on the back of the drawing to see if the student is correct.
8) Students repeat steps 6 and 7 with Student B looking at Student A's drawing.
9) Students find another partner and repeat steps 6-8.
10) Students continue until time is up.

Variation:
1) After students have looked at each other's pictures and discussed them, in plenary, the teacher draws a house on the board (wherever there is space) and asks one student to come up and draw one of the nouns listed on the board.
2) The student must use the noun and its location in a sentence (Example: The chair is in the living room.).
3) When the first student is done, the teacher calls up another student and asks the student to complete step 2, but use a different noun and a different preposition.
4) Teacher continues to call on students until all students have had a chance, or all nouns and prepositions have been used.

4.17 Error Analysis

Level: Intermediate

Goal: To review use of prepositions of location and analyze mistakes

Repetition PhraseS: The students repeat aloud the sentences that correctly describe the picture.

Special Materials: Each student in each group must have a piece of paper, and if possible, the teacher should provide a large piece of paper to each group.

Procedure:
1) Students are divided into groups of 3-4.
2) In each group, the teacher gives students a large piece of paper.
3) One student in each group must draw a location (like a house, apartment building, a park, a lake, a field, a swimming pool, etc...).
4) The rest of the students in each group must brainstorm at least 10 nouns to add to the picture.
5) Each student in the group is assigned to draw 2-3 of the nouns in the picture.
6) As a group, students look at their picture and write on another separate piece of paper a sentence describing the location of each of the nouns in their picture.
7) Students must underline their prepositions. Students must repeat their sentences aloud.
8) When students have written 10 correct sentences about their picture, the teacher comes to check if the sentences are correct.
9) If the sentences are incorrect, students must correct them together.
10) If the sentences are correct, students must choose 5 and write them on another piece of paper.
11) Students then try to write 5 more sentences about their picture, but the sentences must be describing incorrect locations of the nouns. For example, if the flowers are under the window, students would write "The flowers are over the window."
12) When all the groups have written their 5 correct and 5 incorrect sentences, students must post their picture and sentences together on the wall. Students must give their picture a name, and write the name on top of the picture.

13) Each group must get another piece of paper and write all the names of the pictures on separate lines.
14) All groups walk around the room together looking at the pictures, and trying to decide which sentences describing the picture are correct, and which are incorrect.
15) In each group, one person records the numbers of the incorrect sentences that the group has decided on, and writes a correct sentence next to it.
16) When all groups have completed step 15, in plenary, the teacher calls on each group to report the incorrect sentences for each picture, and groups compare answers and correct the incorrect sentences together.

Variation:
1) Students complete the activity same as above, except that they start with writing sentences in each group.
2) Each group must write 10 sentences using various nouns and prepositions.
3) As a group, students draw the picture to illustrate the sentences, but put 5 of the nouns in the wrong place, so the sentence about them is incorrect.
4) Students then post their pictures and sentences around the room, and students must guess which of the pictures are incorrect and don't go with the sentences.

4.18 Adjectives

Level: Beginning-Advanced

Goal: To review adjectives and use in context

Repetition Phrase: Student A = I am wearing a blue jacket and dark glasses. Student B = Find someone wearing a blue jacket and dark glasses. This will vary according to descriptions. Or for more advanced students: Student A = I am a very shallow, egotistical lawyer, dressed in a dark suit. Student B = Find a shallow, egotistical lawyer dressed in a dark suit.

Special Materials: Students will need to bring a small pack of self-hardening clay, or play-dough. Students will have a lot left over and need to save the clay or play-dough for future use in class. Students are welcome to pool money to purchase one pack for several students and share it.

Procedure:
1) Teacher instructs students to write a description of any person, real or make-believe, using the adjectives students are currently studying in class. Students are to make two copies of the description. Teacher should model this on the board. One should say "I am _____" and the other should be "Find someone _____. Both of the descriptions should be the same, but have different beginnings.
2) Teacher circulates and helps students and corrects grammar.
3) Teacher collects the descriptions and put half of them in a pile, and leaves the other half in a separate place. Teacher must be careful not to separate the pairs of sentences.
4) Teacher re-distributes the papers so that each student gets either the "I am" description or the "Find" description. Teacher must be careful that students don't receive their own description.
5) Students must now make the person in the description out of clay or play-dough, and repeat the repetition phrase while doing so. Students write the repetition phrase on the back.
6) When students are done, they walk around the room with their drawing and try to find someone who has a similar drawing.
7) When students find the person with a similar drawing, students share their repetition phrases with each other to make sure they got the correct match. Students must ask each other questions to verify that they have the correct person. Teacher should model these questions on the board.

    Example: "Is your person egotistical and shallow?"
    "Is your person wearing a dark suit?"

8) Students line up in pairs at the front of the room, and take turns sharing their sculptures and reading their repetition phrases.
9) If time, teacher distributes the other half of the descriptions (the ones that were not used) giving one to each student. Each student should have either "I am looking for…" or "I am ….."
10) Students must ask each other questions in order to find the person who has their match.

11) When students have correctly matched the descriptions, they line up in front and read the descriptions aloud and share their sculptures.

Variation:
1) Teacher can review descriptive adjectives being learned at the moment with students first.
2) Teacher writes her own descriptions making sure to have a "I am...." "and an "I'm looking for...." version of each sentence.
3) Teacher distributes the sentences (best if given in small strips of paper) to students and students follow steps 5-8.

4.19 Modals

Level: Intermediate

Goal: To review recent vocabulary, and the use of the modal "can".

Repetition Phrases: *boots*
You can wear them when there is snow.
You can wear them on your feet.
They can keep your feet warm.
(students will make up their own sentences according to the vocabulary word they are assigned.)

Procedure:
1) Teacher assigns each student a vocabulary word they have been learning in the text.
2) Teacher models a word on the board, and shows students how to write sentences about the word using "can". Use repetition phrases as example.
3) Teacher instructs students to draw a picture of their word.
4) Students must try to think of the repetition phrases as they draw.
5) When students have completed their drawings, the teacher asks for one volunteer to leave the room.
6) Another volunteer comes to the front of the room with his/her drawing, and holds it up for the class.
7) In plenary, the students try to think of three sentences using "can" about that student's word.

8) The student volunteer writes the sentences on the board.
9) The student that is outside the classroom is called to come in.
10) The student with the picture hides the picture from the student that was outside, and reads the clues to the student.
11) The student must guess what the word is.
12) When the student has guessed what the word is, the other student shows that student the picture and repeats the word and repetition phrases again.
13) Teacher asks for another volunteer and repeats steps 5-12.

Variation 1:
Students may work in groups and each group does one word and writes three repetition phrases about it.

Variation 2:
Students may complete steps 1-6, but then the student at the board writes his/her own sentences on the board, and the other students must correct them first, and then call the student in from outside.

Variation 3:
The students complete steps 1-5, and then work in pairs and try to guess each other's words. Students line up to share their words and phrases at the end of the class.

4.20 Passive

Level: Advanced

Goal: To review the passive and use it in context, speaking

Repetition Phrases: These will be the sentences students have written in the passive, about the picture. EXAMPLE: The meal was delivered to the client.
The soup was brought to the girl.
The meal was served.

Procedure:
1) Students are divided into groups of four – six (no more than 4 groups altogether) and given a piece of poster paper (or students are told to bring the poster paper the day before).

2) Students are instructed to work together drawing (markers work well) a picture with a lot of activity. Students are encouraged to choose a theme for the picture according to the chapter they are working on in the book.
3) Teacher collects the drawings and re-distributes them to different groups.
4) Students are instructed to write a specific number of sentences in the passive, about the drawing. Students work together in their groups, and need to repeat each sentence they write together, aloud (repetition phrases).
5) The groups then write their sentences on the board.
6) The students are given 10 minutes to go to the board and try to make any corrections necessary to any group's sentences.
7) When students have finished, teacher checks for accuracy, and discusses any remaining mistakes with the students.

Variation:
1) Students are assigned to write (individually) a paragraph in the passive, about the drawings.
2) Teacher then collects the paragraphs, checks them, and prepares an error analysis worksheet for students (he/ she types out the incorrect sentences and distributes them).
3) Students work in groups to correct the mistakes.

4.21 Comparatives/Superlatives

Level: Beginning – intermediate

Goal: To review comparatives and superlatives

Repetition Phrase: My picture is (more)_____ than the others.
My picture is the (most) _____ picture.

Procedure:
1) Teacher reviews a recent vocabulary list. Teacher reviews the rules for comparatives/superlatives.
2) In plenary, students choose a favorite word from the list that is easy to draw or paint.

3) Students paint a picture of the word. They are told to think of how they can make their painting different from the others (they are all painting the same thing).
4) While painting, the students should be thinking of how their painting is different, and repeating aloud the repetition phrases filling them in with correct form of the superlative or the comparative.

    Example: My picture is the saddest picture.
                      My picture is sadder than the others.
                      My picture is more beautiful than the others.
                      My picture is the most beautiful picture.

The teacher may want to have students fill in the repetition phrases with what they are actually painting or drawing:

    Example: My rose is the brightest rose in the class.

5) When students are done drawing, they are divided into groups of four.
6) Students share their paintings/drawings and come up with 5 sentences using the comparative, and five sentences using the superlative for any of the pictures in the group.
7) Students choose a representative from the group to report their sentences to the class, while the other students in the group hold up their artwork for the others to see.

Variation:
1) After students have completed steps 1-7, have them design categories for the drawings like: the funniest, the most interesting, the most thought-provoking, the most unusual, the most daring, the most flamboyant, etc...
2) The teacher (or a chosen student) writes these categories on the board.
3) Students put a title on their artwork.
4) Students cruise around the room looking at the artwork and selecting pictures for each category.
5) Students write the name of the artwork they chose, under the category they think it should win. If more than one person lists a particular picture for a particular category, points can be tabulated underneath the title.
6) Students tally the points and see who the winners are under each category.

7) A student chosen as the announcer announces the winning artwork by its category (EX: The most ambiguous picture of a rose, goes to _____ by _____).

4.22 Comparatives / Works of Art

Level: Intermediate -Advanced

Goal: To review comparatives, speaking fluency, writing practice.

Repetition Phrase: Students must be thinking or saying sentences comparing their artwork to the original while they are drawing.

Special Materials: Teachers may provide each student with a picture of a famous (or not famous) work of art OR students should be assigned to get a picture of a work of art from the library, book of their own, or internet.

Procedure:
1) Students are assigned as homework to try to make a copy of their work of art to the best of their ability.
2) Students bring the copies and the original pictures to class the next day.
3) Teacher reviews comparison words with students such as more than, less than, taller, shorter, more beautiful, etc.
4) Students are divided into groups of 3-4 students and choose one student's artwork to write comparisons about.
5) Students choose one person to write the sentences down for the group.
6) Students are given 10 minutes to compare the student artwork to the original.
7) When time is called, the teacher checks each group's work, and gives each group one point for each CORRECT sentence.
8) The group with the most points wins.
9) Students then form two lines facing each other, and bring their artwork and the originals.
10) Students take turns showing their artwork and telling their partner five sentences comparing their own artwork to the original.
11) Students in one line all move to the right one person, so everyone has a new partner.

12) Repeat steps 10 and 11 until students are back in the same spot where they started in the line.
13) Teacher assigns students to write down their five comparison sentences as homework..
14) The next day in class, students post up their artwork and sentences next to the originals, and walk around the class reading each other's sentences and looking at the artwork.

Variation:
1) If time is limited, students can complete Steps 1-3 and then write five sentences comparing their own picture to the original.
2) Students then complete steps 9-11.

4.23 Comparatives/Superlatives: The Bachelor/ The Bachelorette

* Adapted from ABC's "The Bachelor/ The Bachelorette"

Level: Intermediate-Advanced

Goal: To review use of comparatives and superlatives

Repetition Phrase: She is better for you because she is _____er, _____er, and more_____. OR He is better for you because he is _____er, _____er, and more _____. He is the most _____ of all the contestants. (fill in blanks with adjectives in the comparison or superlative form).

Procedure:
1) Teacher tells students they will play "The Bachelor" and "The Bachelorette". One female student must volunteer to be the bachelorette, and one male student must volunteer to be the bachelor.
2) Girls are grouped on one side of the room, and boys (or men) on the other.
3) Girls must draw or paint a picture of who they think would be a perfect match for their bachelor. While drawing students must say aloud the repetition phrases, then write them on the back of the paper. Students must

use at least two comparatives and one superlative in their explanation of why their person would be an ideal match for the bachelor.
4) Boys complete step 3, drawing or painting the perfect match for the bachelorette.
5) While the girls and boys are preparing their contestants, the bachelor and bachelorette must write what kind of woman or man they are looking for, and which qualities they admire in the opposite sex.
6) While the girls and boys are still working on their drawings, the bachelor and bachelorette take turns announcing the qualities they are looking for, and the other students have a chance to make some changes to their repetition phrases and artwork.
7) The bachelor and bachelorette may join the boy and girl teams to help them with their comparative sentences while they finish.
8) When all students have completed their artwork, the bachelorette or bachelor stands at the front of the room, and each boy takes turns showing their contestant and reading why their contestant would be the best match.
9) The bachelor then stands at the front and the girls take turns showing their contestant and reading why their contestant would be the best match.
10) Students line up their contestants (the artwork) around the room and students vote for the best match for the bachelor and the best match for the bachelorette.
11) When votes have been tabulated, the winners read their descriptions again, and the happy couple's pictures are posted in front of the room.

4.24 Simple Past Review

Level: Intermediate-Advanced

Goal: To review the simple past, especially spelling, and irregular verbs

Repetition Phrases: Students will say aloud the sentence they wrote and illustrated with their assigned verb.

Procedure:
1) Teacher divides students into groups of two, and each pair goes to the board together.
2) Each pair of students must make two columns side by side and number up to ten (or whatever number of students there are in the class) in each column. Each PAIR has two columns, NOT each student.
3) Teacher dictates any verbs he/she thinks students need to work on. One student writes the verb (in the present tense) and the other student checks their work.
4) Teacher circulates and corrects mistakes or has students correct their own mistakes.
5) The other student in each pair now writes (in the second column) the past tense of each verb, and his/her partner checks his/her work.
6) Students return to their seats.
7) Teacher assigns each student a verb to illustrate.
8) Students must think of a sentence using that verb in the past tense, and illustrate the sentence.
9) Students write the sentence on the back of the illustration, and repeat it aloud (repetition phrase).
10) Teacher collects the drawings.
11) Students return to the board in pairs.
12) Student A turns and faces the board, and the Student B stands with his/her back to the board, facing his/her partner.
13) Student A reads the verb in the present tense, and Student B says the past tense of that verb.
14) Continue until all verbs have been said in the past tense.
15) Partners exchange places.
16) Repeat step 13 with Student B reading the present tense.
17) Students switch places again, and this time Student A reads the past tense and Student B must say the present.
18) Repeat step 17 with Student B reading the past tense.
19) Students return to their seats, but don't erase the board.
20) Teacher holds up a drawing of one of the verbs, and students must guess the verb and shout out the past tense.
21) Continue until all drawings have been shown, or time is up.

4.25 Making Suggestions/ Giving Compliments

Level: Intermediate-Advanced

Goal: To practice giving advice to each other and using the modals could and should.

Repetition Phrase: You should.... You could.... You should have... (w/ simple past of verb) and You could have.... I like .....

Procedure:
1) Teacher directs students to walk around the building or campus for 10 minutes looking for inspiration for a painting.
2) When students return, they are given 15 minutes to paint anything they feel like.
3) Teacher reviews giving suggestions. Students brainstorm sentences using should, should have, could, could have and teacher writes them on the board. Teacher must be careful to clarify that suggestions with could have and should have are referring to the past while sentences with could and should are referring to the present.
4) Teacher reviews how to give compliments and asks students to brainstorm compliments for a painting. Teacher (or students) write the possible compliments on the board.
5) Teacher divides class into two. Students in Group A lay their paintings out on their desks, and students in Group B go to a Group A student's desk and look at the painting.
6) Each student from Group B must give the student from Group B two suggestions regarding their painting, and two compliments.
7) Students from Group B go from student to student until they have given suggestions and compliments to all Group A students.
8) Now Group B students display their paintings and stand behind them. Students from Group A now repeat steps 6-8.

Variation:
* Painting is the most fun for this kind of activity, but teachers who don't have proper facilities or students with access to paints and a sink may want to use an easier medium such as crayons or markers.

4.26 Conditionals
Untrue (Contrary to Fact) in the Present/Future

Level: Intermediate-Advanced

Goal: To review conditional sentences untrue in the present/future using If .... were or simple past of verb, with would.

Repetition Phrase: Students should repeat the sentence they have completed.

>   Example: If I were a teacher, I wouldn't give my students any homework.

Procedure:
1) Teacher writes an example sentence on the board. Here are some suggestions;

   If she were a student, she would never turn in her work on time.
   If I won the lottery, I would buy all my friends a new car.
   If they went to Hawaii, they would never leave their hotel room.

2) Teacher asks students to tell him/her what kind of sentences they are.

   Answer: Conditional: Untrue in the present/future.

3) Teacher asks students to write the first clause in a sentence (the if clause) and not write the second clause. The clause should be written at the top of a blank piece of drawing paper from their sketch pads. Teacher should write an example on the board like If I were the president... or If they wrote a book......
4) Teacher mingles and checks that students are only writing the first part of the sentence, and that the grammar is correct (careful that students using the verb to be use were instead of was).
5) Teacher collects the papers and re-distributes them to different students. Students must finish the clause at the bottom of the paper, and illustrate it.
6) While students are finishing the sentences and drawing (or painting), the teacher circulates to check grammar and make sure students are repeating or talking about their sentences in the target language.

7) When most students have finished, teacher calls time and tells students they must find the person who wrote the beginning of their sentence. Teacher asks students what questions they could ask in order to find that person. (Example: Did you write If I were the president...? Or Is this the clause you wrote?). Teacher writes these questions on the board.
8) Teacher then asks students how they would ask the other student how they would have ended the sentence. (Example: How would you have finished this sentence?). Teacher writes this question on the board.
9) Teacher directs students to walk around and find the person that wrote the beginning of their sentence. The student who wrote the end of the sentence (Student B) then shows the other student (Student A) the end, and his/her illustration. Student B asks the questions from Step 8.
10) When Student A has answered the question, Student A shows Student B his/her drawing and reads the sentence. If Student A has Student B's clause, then both students repeat Steps 9 and 10. If Student A has someone else's sentence, Student A and B look for another partner.
11) Continue until everyone has had a chance to meet with the person who had the end of their sentence.
12) Students line up in front of the class with their drawings and sentences and take turns reading them aloud. Teacher and students correct any grammar mistakes not corrected previously.

REFERENCES

Azar, B. (2002). Understanding and Using English Grammar, Third Edition. White Plains, N.Y.: Pearson Education.

Hess, N. & Pollard, L. (1997). Zero Prep; Ready to Use Activities for the Language Classroom. Burlingame, CA: Alta Books.

Woodward, S. (1997). Fun With Grammar; Communicative Activities for the Azar Grammar Series. Upper Saddle river, N.J.: Prentice-Hall, Inc.

Chapter Five

Speaking Activities

5.1 Speaking Chain

Level: Intermediate – Advanced

Goal: To review vocabulary, speaking

Repetition Phrase: This is a _____. (Complete with name of word student has illustrated).

Procedure:
1) Each student is assigned one vocabulary word to illustrate.
2) While illustrating the word, the student must say the repetition phrase aloud or to him/herself.
3) Students sit in a circle.
4) One student is appointed the challenger, and writes the student responses on the board. At any time, the challenger may stop the students and ask why they chose the word they did. Students must provide an explanation.
5) The first student holds up his/her drawing and says the repetition phrase.
6) The student to the left says the first thing that comes to his/her mind when looking at the drawing and hearing the word.

   Example: One student might say " This is a sun." The following student might say, "hot" and the next student "beach" and the next student "swim".

7) This continues until all students have had a turn. Then, another student holds up his/her drawing, and students start the chain again.
8) Continue until time is up, or all students have had a chance to hold up their drawings.

Variation:
1) Complete steps 1-4.
2) Teacher collects all the drawings.
3) Teacher chooses one and holds it up, and appoints a student to start the chain.
4) Students complete steps 6-9, with the teacher holding up a new drawing each time.

5.2 Conversation Line with a Picture

Level: Intermediate –Advanced

Goal: Speaking, sharing opinions, asking questions

Repetition Phrase: Students repeat aloud what they are drawing.

Procedure:
1) Students are instructed to draw or paint a picture of a current event, or a subject that is interesting to them, and that they have an opinion about. Teachers should review words that show opinions like "I think" "I believe" "In my opinion", etc… Teachers might want to give a theme similar to what they are currently covering in the textbook.
2) While drawing or painting, students say aloud the items they are putting into the picture.
3) Students make two lines facing each other.
4) Student A looks at Student B's picture and asks what the picture is about. Student B answers and explains the picture. The two students discuss the event in the picture and give their opinions about it.
5) Student B looks at Student A's picture and repeats step 4.
6) The student on the far left of one of the lines (teacher decides which line) goes all the way to the other end of the line, and the other students move down one so that everyone has a new partner.
7) Repeat steps 4-6 until students in the moving line are back to their original place.

Variation:
1) Students complete steps 1-2, then the teacher collects all the pictures.
2) The teacher chooses one picture for all students to discuss.
3) Each time students move the teacher holds up a different picture.
4) Students may use pictures from magazines or the internet instead of drawing them, but they should cut them out and glue them onto a piece of drawing paper. While doing this they should be thinking or saying aloud what is happening in the picture.

5.3 Beginning, Middle, and End

Level: Intermediate – Advanced

Goal: To review vocabulary, listening, writing, speaking

Special Materials: Four large pieces of white poster paper

Repetition Phrase: Students repeat aloud what it is they are drawing.

Procedure:
1) Teacher divides students into 3 groups.
2) Students in each group are given a large piece of poster paper.
3) Each group is told to discuss what they would like to put in their picture, and then work together to draw a picture. Students repeat aloud what they are drawing as they draw it. (Markers are suggested for this activity)
4) After each group has drawn their picture, the teacher collects the pictures and re-distributes them. Each group now has a new picture.
5) Students in each group must look carefully at the new pictures, and discuss what it is they see in the picture, trying to memorize as much as possible.
6) Teacher collects drawings and re-distributes again, so that each group has now seen all three pictures. Repeat step 5.
7) Each group writes a story that includes all three pictures. One picture should be chosen as the beginning, one as the middle, and one as the end. Students work together to write the same story. Only one person should do the writing, while the others help and correct the writer's grammar/spelling.
8) When all groups have written their stories, each group hands in their story to the teacher. Students then mingle around the room looking for someone from a different group.
9) Students try to tell their story to another student. If needed they can go to the teacher to look at their story one more time, but they cannot READ the story that was written, they must re-tell it in their own words.
10) Continue until students have had a chance to tell their stories at least three times.
11) Teacher posts the three stories and the three pictures, and students take turns reading them and looking at the pictures.

5.4 What Happened in the Picture?

Level: Intermediate – Advanced

Goal: To review all tenses in context, to practice telling stories, expansion of vocabulary

Repetition Phrase: Students summarize what happened in their picture in one or two sentences.

Procedure:
1) Students are told to think of a recent event that happened to them, that would be easy to illustrate.
2) Students illustrate their event, repeating aloud the repetition phrase as they draw.
3) Students find a partner and take turns sharing what happened in their pictures.
4) Students find another partner and this time share what happened in their story AND their first partner's story.
5) Students find another partner and this time, share what happened in their story AND their FIRST TWO partners' stories.

Variation 1:
1) Instead of sharing their stories, the students find partners and Student A asks Student B questions about their story.

    Example: "What happened here?" "Why is she smiling?" Etc…

2) Student B answers the questions and helps Student A understand his/her story.
3) Repeat steps 1-2 with Student B asking the questions.
4) Repeat steps 1-3 with new partners.
5) Continue until time is up, or students have met with at least 10 different partners.

Variation 2:
1) Teacher divides the class in two. The first group of students posts their drawings around the room and stands by them.

2) The second group finds a person standing by their drawing, and listens to their story.
3) Teacher calls time, and all students move down one (all students should have a new partner) and the students standing by their drawings tell their story to their new partner.
4) Students continue until students from group 2 have seen all the drawings from group 1.
5) Students from group 2 now post their drawings and stand by them.
6) Students from group 1 complete steps 2 – 4.

5.5 Categories

Level: Intermediate – Advanced

Goal: To review and expand vocabulary, speaking

Repetition Phrases: These are things that _____. (fall, break, ring, you can do with your hands, etc...) Students also repeat the names of the pictures they cut out.

Special Materials: The class will complete steps 1-3 together (at the end of class), then the teacher will assign students steps 4-5. Students will need magazines, glue, and paper. The next day in class, students will complete the activity finishing steps 6-12 .

Procedure:
1) Teacher writes a list of words on the board : EXAMPLE: glass, window, foot, heart, spirit. Teacher then says "What category would you put these words in ?"
2) Students must try to guess the category. If students can't answer, teacher gives them the answer (things you can break). Teacher writes another set of words on the board. EXAMPLE: watch T.V., cry, sleep, wink, stare, squint.
3) Students try to guess the category (things you can do with your eyes).
4) Students are assigned a collage as homework. Students must choose a category (this could be with verbs (things you can do ...), adjectives (things that are hot) or nouns (things are hot or cold). Students find items

that fit into the category from magazines or the internet, and cut them out (print them first, if from the internet) and glue them onto the collage.
5) Students must repeat the repetition phrases while making the collages. Students write the name of the category on the back of the collage.
6) Students bring their collages to class the next day.
7) Students are divided into groups of 3-4 students.
8) Students take turns holding up their pictures and telling the other students the names of the pictures in the collage. Students in the group repeat the names of the pictures.
9) Students in the group try to guess the category. When they have guessed correctly, the next student has a turn.
10) Students continue until all students in each group have had a chance to share their collages.
11) Each group chooses the most difficult category to guess and that person brings their collage to the front of the room.
12) In plenary, students repeat the names of the words in the collages as students hold them up, and try to guess the category (students in that person's group cannot guess).

Variation:
1) Class completes steps 1-2 together.
2) Students are divided into teams.
3) Teacher writes an example of a category on the board (like "Things that are yellow") and students in the group work together to draw a quick picture of a yellow item, label it, and hold it up. The group who holds up a correct item first, gets a point.

5.6 What Am I?

Level: Beginning – Advanced

Goal: To review and expand vocabulary, increase fluency, writing

Repetition Phrase: I am blue, I am round, I am juicy. What am I ? (a blueberry)

Procedure:
1) Teacher gives students a set of clues. EXAMPLE: I am tall. I have a long neck. I am an animal. What am I ?
2) Students guess the animal (giraffe).
3) Students must choose a noun to describe, and draw or paint a picture of the noun.
4) While drawing or painting, students must repeat aloud the repetition phrases, and write them on the back.
5) Students are divided into teams.
6) Each team sends one person to the board.
7) Teacher collects the drawings or paintings, and chooses one, and reads the clues written on the back (without letting students see the picture).
8) Students compete to see who can guess the noun correctly, and write the name of the noun on the board correctly the fastest. The team who gets the word written correctly first gets a point.

Variation:
1) Students can use clay or play-dough to make the answer to the riddles.

5.7 Self-Portraits

Level: Beginning – Intermediate

Goal: Speaking, to review the use of descriptive adjectives

Repetition Phrase: I am a _____, _____, and _____ woman. OR I am a _____, _____, and _____ man. (or boy or girl)

Special Materials: Students will need to bring some kind of small mirror, such as a compact mirror.

Procedure:
1) Students review a list of adjectives (these can be very simple like pretty, tall, young, or for more advanced students; loquacious, altruistic, energetic, etc…).

2) Students are told to look into their mirrors and think about the list they just reviewed. They need to think of three of those words that would describe themselves.
3) Students must paint or draw their own self- portrait, trying to represent those three words somehow in their drawing. The teacher might want to show some famous portraits from a website or bring some from home as an example.
4) Students must say the repetition phrase with the three adjectives describing themselves inserted into the sentence while they are drawing/painting.
5) After students have finished their artwork, they get up and find a partner.
6) Student A must try to guess Student B's three adjectives and say "You are a _____, _____, and _____ man/woman.
7) When Student A guesses the right adjectives, Student B completes step 6.
8) When both students have completed step 6, the students find a new partner.
9) Students continue steps 5-8 until the teacher calls time.

Variation:
1) Students complete steps 1-9 with only one change. Instead of choosing three words that describe themselves, they choose two that describe themselves that they can represent in the picture, and one that is false, and does not describe themselves.
2) After step 9, students display their portraits on the wall (or on the desks) and students walk around looking once more at all the portraits before they sit down.
3) In plenary, each student comes to the front of the class and holds up their portrait and says their repetition phrase.
4) Students must choose which adjective is false. The student holding up their artwork must then tell them if they are correct or not, and explain why.

5.8 Art Show

Level: Beginning – Advanced

Goal: To review comparatives and superlatives, practice fluency

Repetition Phrase: This is my best picture because _____. This is my worst picture because _____.

Special Materials: Throughout the quarter or semester, students should be saving all the artwork produced in class. At the end of the quarter or semester, students are asked to choose their best and worst pictures produced, and bring them to class. Teacher needs to find a way for students to display these pictures either in the classroom, or hall or bulletin board somewhere in the building for all students to look at. Teacher might want to prepare the titles "Our Best" and "Our Worst" and have students post their pictures under those headings when they come in.

Procedure:
1) Students are assigned to choose their best and worst pictures made throughout the semester. While looking at their artwork, students repeat the repetition phrases filling in the reasons why they chose those particular pictures.
2) Students bring their chosen pictures to class and form two lines facing each other.
3) The students facing each other are partners.
4) Teacher designates one line to hold up their pictures for their partners.
5) The person in the other line asks the students questions about their partner's work. Teacher might want to model these questions on the board before the activity begins. EXAMPLES: Why did you choose this as your best? Why did you choose this one as your worst? Why don't you like it? Why do you like it?, etc,,
6) The student answers the questions and makes sure to include the repetition phrases.
7) Now students in the opposite line share their pictures and answer their partners' questions about the pictures.
8) The person on the far left of one line (chosen by the teacher) moves down to the far right of the line, and all other students in that line move one to the left. Now everyone has a new partner.
9) Repeat steps 4-7.
10) Repeat step 8, and continue until all students are in the same place they started.
11) Students are now asked to display their artwork as indicated by the teacher.
12) Students are allowed to walk around and look at the artwork and discuss it with each other (this works best with more advanced students). Stu-

dents are encouraged to discuss what the pictures are about, and what was the goal of the activity to produce that particular picture. Students are also encouraged to use comparatives and superlatives while discussing the artwork (example:That one is prettier than the first one. This one is the funniest one.)

Variation:
1) Students complete steps 1-12.
2) Students choose categories such as "Most Interesting" "Most Unusual" "Most original", and write the titles on the board.
3) Students then walk around looking at each of the pictures again and nominate them for the various categories (teachers can put a post-it note next to each picture and students write the category on the note, and then students who agree add a point under that category).
4) Teacher adds up the points and announces the winners.

5.9 Puppet Show

Level: Beginning- Advanced

Goal: Speaking, review of specific vocabulary or fluency practice

Repetition Phrase: Students imagine what their puppet's personality would be like and say the adjectives describing the puppet out loud while they are making it.

Special Materials: Students are encouraged to use whatever materials they have available. Suggested materials are old socks, buttons, yarn, paper, stickers, pasta, beans, raisins, etc...

Procedure:
1) Students are assigned to make puppets the day before class.
2) Students may use any materials, but sock puppets are easiest.
3) While making the puppet, students must imagine the puppet's name (must be a name in the target language) and what the puppet's personality is like. Students repeat this aloud while creating the puppet.
4) Students bring puppets to class the next day.

5) Students are divided into groups of 3 or 4 students and given 15-30 minutes to create a short dialog (for beginners – use what they have learned up to that point, for more advanced students give them a theme from the chapter they are studying like food, transportation, etc…).
6) Students practice together.
7) Each group presents their puppet presentation in front of the class. Ideally, students can create a little puppet stage in the classroom by going behind the teacher's desk or any other easily constructed stage.
8) Students and teacher discuss each presentation after it has been performed.

5.10 T.V. Talk

Level: Intermediate- Advanced

Goal: To review vocabulary involving T.V. and movies, and to increase fluency and writing skills.

Repetition PhraseS: This character is from the show _____. He or she is _____, _____ and _____. This episode was about _____.

Special Materials: Students will need to watch a T.V. show or movie in the target language. Preferably, students can do this the class before this activity is to be executed. If students do not have access to T.V. or movies in the target language, they may use the internet. If students do not have internet access, it is advisable for teachers to show a T.V. show or movie in class. Students will need one set of play-dough or clay.

Procedure:
1) Students are assigned to watch one T.V. show or movie in the target language (see special materials above). This must be done before this activity will be executed.
2) After watching the show, students will choose their favorite character and re-create it out of play-dough or clay.
3) Students will write on a separate piece of paper, the repetition phrases. While they are making the character, they need to be saying these phrases out loud, and then writing them.

4) Students bring their character to class.
5) Students are divided into two groups.
6) The first group stands in a circle facing out.
7) The second group stands in a circle facing the inner circle. Every student should be facing another student
8) Students in the inner circle hold up their clay/play-dough creations and read or say in their own words their repetition phrases.
9) Students in the inner circle do the talking while students in the outer circle listen.
10) It is important that students do NOT stop talking even when they are done. They must continue to talk until teacher calls time.
11) When teacher calls time, students in the outer circle move one person to the right. Now all students have a new partner.
12) Repeat steps 8-11.
13) Repeat steps 8-12 until all students in the outside circle have listened to all students in the inner circle.
14) Change circles so that the outer circle is now inside, and doing the talking while the other students are now doing the listening.
15) Repeat steps 8-13.

VariationS:
1) Teacher can show movie or T.V. show in class instead of students watching on their own.
2) If time is limited, and /or there is a large class, students can do the talking and listening 2-3 times before changing circles instead of listening/talking with all the students.

5.11 Let's Talk Politics

Level: Advanced

Goal: To increase fluency, to review vocabulary related to politics, social values

Repetition Phrases: Students need to say aloud the ideas they are pasting into their collages. For example, if a student includes a picture of a politician being arrested, the student must say aloud their political viewpoint about this (such as; I am against political corruption).

Procedure:

1) Students must bring political magazines and newspapers to class.
2) Teacher should review with students political vocabulary. Teachers may want to give students a list of words involving social and political issues such as the following words;

   - corruption, middle-class, upper-class, left, right, center, civil rights, environment,
   - dictatorship, democracy, political party, taxes, laws, speech, government,
   - citizens, police clash, 0press, bomb, criminal, explosion, reporter, newscast, coup
   - d'etat, weapon, leader, minister, movement, president, income, poverty, prejudice,
   - racism, terrorism, immigration, illiteracy, AIDS, discrimination, civil liberties,
   - malnutrition, hunger, war, rape, controversy, etc...

3) Teacher and students discuss words and their meanings.
4) Teacher tells students they are going to make a collage using photos from the magazines they brought. The collages must express each student's political opinions/viewpoints on various current issues.
5) While students are making their collages they must say aloud their viewpoints as they cut and glue the pictures.
6) When teacher calls time, students write next to their pictures their viewpoint on that issue.
7) Students are asked to mingle around the room and find a partner. They must ask questions about each other's pictures and try to understand each other's viewpoints. They are NOT to agree or disagree, but just understand what each student's viewpoints are on various issues.
8) When the teacher calls time (or rings a bell, whatever sign she/he uses to say time is up), students change partners and repeat Step 7.
9) When time is up, teacher calls on students to tell the class about one political viewpoint of ANOTHER student.
10) Teacher continues until all students have had a chance to tell about at least one other student's political viewpoint/s.

5.12 International Inventor

Adapted from ABC's "American Inventor"

Level: Intermediate-Advanced

Goal: To practice giving speeches in the target language, to increase fluency

Repetition PhraseS: Students practice saying the name of their invention and what it does.

Special Materials: Necessary: Students must have at home materials to make an invention such as tinker toys, blocks, metal, sticks, clay, anything the students can find at home to build a small-scale model of their invention. **Optional:** A video camera to film the presentations, and a computer with a class web-site so students can view the presentations again and vote online.

Procedure:
1) Teacher tells students they will be contestants on a new TV show called "International Inventor". Students will be competing to see who can create the most useful and original invention.
2) Teacher asks students to brainstorm in groups what they think are the top 5 inventions of the last ten years.
3) Students share their groups' inventions with the class.
4) Teacher ask students what characteristics those inventions had in order to be successful (Example: useful, create less work for humans, fun).
5) Teacher tells students to put their heads down and try to think of an invention they think would possess all of those characteristics.
6) Students must now draw a picture of their invention. While drawing, students need to be practicing the name of their invention, and what it does.
7) Students are asked to take their inventions home and make a small-scale model. Teacher tells them they can use any materials they can get their hands on like tinker toys, clay, sticks, buttons, whatever they can find.
8) Students must also practice a presentation of their invention including the following points:

   a) name
   b) what it does
   c) why is it necessary

d) how much it would cost to make
e) how much it would cost to buy

9) Students come to class the next day with their inventions and students take turns presenting the inventions to the class, and a panel of judges chosen by the class (about 3 people).

10) Students present their inventions and if possible, they are video-taped. After the presentation the judges may present their scores (from 1-10) according to the criteria listed by the class earlier (useful, fun, creates less work for humans, etc…). Judges and class members may also ask questions and give presenters a chance to clarify.

11) If possible, teacher can post the videos on the class web-site, and give students (the viewers) the chance to vote for their favorite invention. The judges scores and the online voting scores are each worth 50% of the total score. The student with the most points total wins. Also, if it is not possible for students to vote online or even to see the videos, students can vote separately on pieces of paper at the end of all the presentations, and class votes can be worth 50% along with the 50% scores from the judges.

12) The winning student can get help from the teacher in sending in their invention to get a patent through the website www.inventionhome.com or another appropriate website.

References

Hess, N. & Pollard, L. (1997). Zero Prep; Ready to Use Activities for the Language Classroom. Burlingame, CA: Alta Books.

Chapter Six

Listening Activities

6.1 Re-Create the Picture

Level: Beginning- intermediate

Goal: Listening comprehension, following directions in the target language, review of prepositions, adjectives, vocabulary

Repetition Phrase: Students say aloud the names of the objects on their drawing as they draw them.

Procedure:
1) In plenary, review direction words and prepositions such as over, under, right, left, top, bottom, next to, beside, near, far, etc...
2) Teacher has students list 10 nouns they have learned recently in class, on the board.
3) Students are told to make a drawing/ painting incorporating all 10 of those words. Students need to say the words they are drawing as they draw them (see Repetition Phrase).
4) Students are instructed not to look at each other's artwork.
5) Students are divided into pairs and Student A looks at his/her own drawing while Student B gets a blank piece of paper.
6) Student A tries to get Student B to recreate his/her own drawing/painting by telling Student B where everything is in the picture, and giving descriptive adjectives to help with the design of the objects. Student A may NOT, under ANY circumstances, show Student B, his/her painting/drawing.
7) When Student B is finished, Student A shows him/her the real drawing, and they compare.
8) Repeat steps 5-8 with Student B describing their drawing to Student A.

Variation:
1) Students complete steps 1 and 2.
2) Students are assigned a word from the list to draw (dry media is best for this variation).
3) Students repeat the name of what they are drawing as they draw it.
4) A volunteer stands at the front of the room and draws a large rectangle representing a page, on the board.
5) Students are divided into pairs.
6) Student A is instructed to post (using sticky tape or whatever possible to attach the drawings) their drawing and their partner's drawing somewhere on the rectangle. AT THE SAME TIME, Student B is instructed to take out a blank piece of paper and dry media, and turn around, facing the back of the room. Student B may not look at the board.
7) Student A is instructed to look at the board and try to tell Student B how to re-create what is on the board by giving Student B precise directions and using prepositions.
8) After the teacher says time is up, Student B turns around and compares his/her picture to the picture on the board.

9) If time, repeat steps 1-8 having students re-arrange the words on the board, and this time Student B dictates to Student A.
10) Students may also make the words out of construction paper and glue onto a big piece of paper instead of just drawing the words.

6.2 Math Problems

Level: Intermediate – Advanced

Goal: Listening to solve a problem, using language in context, review of numbers

Repetition Phrase: This is the actual word problem the student has created.

Procedure:
1) Teacher gives students an example word problem on the board, and asks them to work in groups to solve the problem.

> Example word problem: John (use a student's name from the class) is having a dinner party tonight. He has invited 7 guests; Mary, Louise, Mark, Luke, Steven, Ann, and Tom. Mary and Tom are married and want to sit together. Mark hates Steven, and Steven is afraid of Luke. Louise is Mary's best friend. John doesn't want to seat himself next to Ann because she never stops talking. Draw a table and put the names of the guests in a seating arrangement that would respect the above criteria.

Possible answers:

1) Students are asked to come up with their own word problem in the target language. Students must repeat aloud the word problem as they write it.
2) Teacher circulates to help students with vocabulary and grammar.
3) After students have written the problem on one side, students must illustrate the answer somehow on the back.
4) Students are divided into groups of 3-4 students.
5) Teacher collects the word problems and distributes one problem to each group.

6) Students work together (TARGET LANGUAGE ONLY!!!) to solve the problem.
7) When they think they have the answer, they check the back of the problem to see the illustrated answer, and check if they are correct.
8) Teacher collects the word problems and re-distributes them.
9) Continue until each group has done about 4-5 problems.
10) Teacher makes each group be a team, and sends one person to the board.
11) Teacher chooses a word problem from the ones she collected but students did not do yet, and dictates it to the students at the board. Students at the board are encouraged to take notes or draw pictures as the teacher is dictating.
12) Teams work together to help their teammate solve the problem. Students should correct each other if any words were heard incorrectly, or not understood.
13) The team that gets the correct answer first, wins the point.
14) Continue until all word problems have been solved.

6.3 Re-tell the story

Level: Intermediate - Advanced

Goal: Listening comprehension, writing, speaking

Repetition PhraseS: Students repeat aloud what they have drawn (their graphic notes from the reading of the story)

Procedure:
1) Teacher selects a short reading the students are familiar with.
2) Teacher tells students he/she will dictate the reading aloud three times. The first time, students must listen only. The second and third times, students must take notes. Notes cannot be written, but must be drawn.
3) After the third reading, students are divided into pairs and given five minutes to say aloud what they have drawn (to each other). These are the repetition phrases.
4) After sharing their drawings and repeating what they've drawn aloud, each pair of students joins another pair of students and tries to re-write the story (one story per group).

5) Each group posts their story on the wall, and students look around and compare stories.
6) Teacher hands out a copy of the story to all students, and students compare their stories to the original version, and discuss unknown vocabulary.

Expansion: (to be completed after Step 6 if there is time)
1) Students are sent to the board in pairs.
2) Each pair of students must number to ten.
3) Teacher dictates ten important verbs from the story.
4) Students write the verbs.
5) Students make another column to the right of their first column, and number 1-10.
6) Students work together to write the past tense of the verbs.
7) In pairs, one students stands with back to the board. The other stands facing his/her partner.
8) The student facing the board reads aloud the first verb, and the student with his/her back to the board (without looking) says the past tense of that verb.
9) Continue until all verbs have been recited in present and past tenses.
10) Students change places so that a different student is now reading the verbs aloud.
11) Continue until all verbs have been read by both students.
12) Now, students change places again, and the student reading the board reads the past tense first, and the student with his/her back to the board says the verb in the present tense.
13) Continue until all verbs have been done, and then students switch places and repeat step 18.
14) The student facing the board now looks at the verbs to help, and tries to re-tell the story to his/her partner.
15) Students switch places and the other student tries to re-tell the story.

6.4 Draw What I Say

Level: Beginning-Advanced

Goal: To follow directions, listening comprehension, prepositions, vocabulary for locations

Repetition Phrase: Students repeat aloud what they have drawn.

Procedure:
1) Teacher dictates a picture for students to draw. Teacher gives locations, colors, everything, and students must try to re-create what the teacher describes.

   Example: On the bottom left of your paper, draw a sun. Make the sun yellow. Put three thin rays coming out of the bottom of the sun. (For more advanced students use more advanced vocabulary; EXAMPLE: Draw a pouty little girl in a blue shirt and red pants, next to a large exotic animal.)

2) Students are divided into groups of four and take turns sharing their drawings and saying aloud what they have drawn and where it is located.
3) Students post their drawings around the room, and compare their drawings with other students.
4) Each student takes their picture down, and returns to his/her desk.
5) Teacher calls out names of items in the picture and asks for volunteers to describe the location of the item, and to describe the item in general (color, size, etc...)

6.5 Art Installation

Level: Beginning- Advanced

Goal: To review concepts for an exam.

Procedure:
1) Students are told at the beginning of the semester that they will be involved in an art installation project (as part of their grade) that they will construct throughout the semester.
2) The idea of the installation will be to learn English from the inside looking out, not from a student looking in at the textbook. The students will be part of the textbook.

3) Groups will be assigned to important concepts to be learned throughout the semester. After each concept has been learned in class, students assigned to the concept are free to begin construction of their installation to review that concept.
4) Installations must include all learning styles– visual, kinesthetic, auditory, and can even include ways to include the senses of smell and taste as well. To do this, students will need access to computers, screens, tape recorders, any technology available.
5) As part of the activity, students should be given the opportunity to visit an installation in a local gallery to get the feel for how installations can be different, or they should be encouraged to visit these websites; artcyclopedia.com, interactive art installations.com, or google "art installations" and check out the many different links under this category.
6) Students are encouraged to have at least three parts to their installation.

   a) Some kind of recorded script with the target vocabulary being used in context (this could be recorded onto a power point presentation, or part of an interactive exercise, or if little technology is available, a simple tape recorder with a student in charge of replaying the tape.
   b) Several forms of visual aid, designed to cover most of the group's designated area for installation (the areas will be specified by the instructor shortly before the installations are put in the classroom). If little or no technology is available, these could be in the form of posters and photographs, if technology is available, ideally students could project their various images on a large screen (or several large screens).
   c) At least one kinesthetic activity where students are able to touch and maneuver target vocabulary or concepts, or use their bodies as part of the activity.

   Example 1: If students are reviewing count-non-count words, a sample activity would be to have a table with many different items on it, like books, pencils, bread, sugar, rice, water, money, CD's and apples. Students must sort the items into count-non-count piles. At the same time, they are being exposed to those same words on the screen, and hearing them out loud from the tape.

Example 2: Students going through the installation must play a game together requiring them to use their bodies. If students are studying the past tense, one student could pull a card from the pile and act out the verb. The other students must guess the verb, and say the past tense. This would happen while they are seeing and hearing the verbs in the background.

    d) Students must design an area for students to write or draw their thoughts and ideas regarding the concept they are working on. This can be in the form of poster paper, or scrolls or wipe off boards, small chalkboards, etc..

7) The week before the exam, students set up their installations in the classroom.
8) Students enter the classroom full of each group's installations and wander about the room going from installation to installation, absorbing the information coming to them visually, and from listening as well as interacting in various ways in each group's project. This is the students' review for their final exam.
9) Students may invite students from other classes to visit their installation. It is recommended to use the installations as much as possible for other students to learn from before taking them down.
10) Students should receive a grade on their project based on the content, organization, effort and creativity of their idea.

References

Hess, N. & Pollard, L. (1997). Zero Prep; Ready to Use Activities for the Language Classroom. Burlingame, CA: Alta Books.

References

Azar, B. (2002). *Understanding and Using English Grammar, Third Edition.* White Plains, N.Y.: Pearson Education.

Hess, N. & Pollard, L. (1997). *Zero Prep; Ready to Use Activities for the Language Classroom.* Burlingame, CA: Alta Books.

Woodward, S. (1997). *Fun With Grammar; Communicative Activities for the Azar Grammar Series.* Upper Saddle river, N.J.: Prentice-Hall, Inc.

http://www.usd.edu/trio/tut/ts/styleres.html (Adapted from Instructor Magazine, 8-89.)

About the Author

Theresa Catalano has a Master's degree in English Language/Linguistics from the University of Arizona and a Bachelor's degree in Elementary Education from the University of Nebraska at Lincoln. She has been a language teacher for more than 15 years, and has taught and/or studied in Pakistan, Turkey, Italy, and the USA. Her teaching experience includes Italian, Spanish, and English as a Second/Foreign Language from the elementary school to the university/community college level. She has also written curriculum for numerous institutions for ESL/EFL programs of the adult education and university level. Besides spending time with her husband and three children, she enjoys the integration of art into her own life in the form of dance, choreography, and painting.

Credits

Editor: Paul Richardson
Cover design by Rosetta Buick
Photography by Rosetta Buick and Eric Scholar
Cover Artwork by Isabella Catalano
Interior Artwork by Theresa and Isabella Catalano
Foreword by Joanne Sowell

www.ingramcontent.com/pod-product-compliance
Lightning Source LLC
Chambersburg PA
CBHW081840170426
43199CB00017B/2792